Praise for *The SOHO Solution*

"The SOHO Solution is a small book with a BIG payoff. This is an easy-to-read, highly practical book where, in 21 short weekly lessons, you can transform your sales results from good to great."

- Dr. Tony Alessandra, author of *The Platinum Rule for Sales Mastery* and *Collaborative Selling*.

"They say, nothing happens until someone sells something. If you're looking to increase your income and happiness as a successful small business owner or sales professional, this book is a must read."

- Dr. Peter Legge, chairman, CEO, publisher, Canada Wide Media Limited and author of *Make Your Life a Masterpiece*.

"The SOHO Solution is the success manual that small business owners and sales professionals have been looking for. I've read scores of books on success in sales and this is one of the most practical and effective ones I've ever seen."

- Jim Cathcart, author of *Relationship Selling* and *The Acorn Principle*.

THE SOHO SOLUTION

THE SOHO SOLUTION:

21 SELLING STRATEGIES FOR GROWING YOUR SMALL BUSINESS

TOM ABBOTT

soho sales coaching

SINGAPORE | CANADA

Published in 2011 by
Soho Sales Coaching Pte. Ltd.
18 Kaki Bukit Road 3 #02-11
Singapore 415978
www.SohoSalesCoaching.com

Author: *Tom Abbott*
Publishing Manager: *Elaine Brindamour Abbott*
Project Editor: *Pam Noda*
Book Designer: *Elaine Brindamour Abbott*

Printed in Singapore

ISBN: 978-0-9730183-1-8

The SOHO Solution may be purchased in bulk for educational, business, fundraising, or sales promotional use. For information, please email prosper@sohosalescoaching.com.

Contents

Foreword

Being a sales trainer can be a tenuous way to make a living. You are constantly reminded of all the old ways people have sold for decades, yet, if you are cutting edge in your approach, you are diligently searching for new success strategies to help your clients go to the next level. It is no longer viable for us to sell our products and services the way they have been sold in the past; the old methods are rapidly becoming obsolete and deemed impotent in today's competitive marketplace. I suggest embracing the newest and best ideas before your competitors do!

The SOHO Solution will be a valuable asset to you in exploring better ways to sell. Tom Abbott teaches you how time-tested techniques and tactics can be used effectively today. He also gives you many new ideas that will help you build more loyal relationships and out-perform your competition.

Occasionally, I read a book straight through in a day or so, underlining key ideas so as to capture the gems as I go. This book is also full of gems, but I suggest you follow the author's advice and take your time reading. Allow yourself to read one chapter per week so that you can digest the ideas and think about how you will integrate them into your selling process. For best results, consider the skills taught, evaluate how they vary from your current strategies and approaches and make action-specific decisions as to how you will manage your sales opportunities going forward. If you do this, I assure you that you will, over time, increase your sales success.

The SOHO Solution addresses many critical aspects of selling today that need to be mastered. Things like fine-tuning your niche so that you can "go to market" with a refreshing, differentiated approach and important skills that will enable you to build relationships and interact more effectively with your prospects. Tom's perspective on product knowledge is the best I have seen— we must be students of ourselves and our competitors to excel in a tough, competitive market.

Above all, I'm convinced that with the methods in this book you will identify more readily with your prospects, enabling you to gain more commitments. If you can enroll more committed buyers and simultaneously build more loyal relationships, you are in a position to thrive in any market.

If you are in sales, this is not a book you will glance through quickly and then loan to a friend. This is a book worthy of your most intrusive study effort. Mark up the margins with your notes, capture and use the best ideas and develop new, highly profitable habits. Then give the book a special place in your library for future (and frequent) reference. You won't want to give this one away!

Don Hutson, co-author of *The One Minute Entrepreneur* and *The One Minute Negotiator*

Preface

I'm writing this book because as a fellow SOHO (small office home office) entrepreneur, it's exactly the book I needed when I started my business more than ten years ago. I'm writing this book for you.

The twenty-one selling strategies introduced in this book address four areas that are essential to achieving success in sales. The four areas are customer fundamentals, product fundamentals, presentation fundamentals and relationship fundamentals.

The strategies introduced in weeks 1 through 6 cover customer fundamentals. These strategies teach you how to save time and money by better understanding your customers and finding more effective ways of reaching them.

Weeks 7 through 11 address the second area, product fundamentals. These strategies deal with the importance of branding yourself and your business.

The third area, presentation fundamentals, is covered in weeks 12 through 16. These strategies teach you how to convert more leads into sales.

Weeks 17 through 21 focus on the fourth area, relationship fundamentals. These strategies demonstrate how your relationship with yourself and others greatly impacts your sales. This book is structured to walk you through the strategies in a certain order, because the sequence has proven to work for me and countless SOHO entrepreneurs around the world. I recommend that you start with the week 1 strategy about discovering your niche and work your way through the strategies in the order that they are presented. If a certain chapter resonates strongly with you right now, however, you're welcome to skip ahead.

At the end of each chapter, you'll find action steps designed to help you apply what you've read, so that you can keep moving forward and begin growing your business immediately. You're also encouraged to visit our website (www.SohoSalesCoaching.com), where you can watch videos and read blog posts that will help you reach your goals faster.

It's my hope that by applying the twenty-one weekly strategies in this book, you'll soon begin attracting your ideal target customer, differentiating yourself in the marketplace and converting more leads into sales.

I would like to express my gratitude to the following people for providing me with support throughout this process.

To my wife, Elaine Brindamour Abbott, because of you, I'm getting to be who I want to be. I love you today, tomorrow and forever.

To my parents, Thomas and Joan Abbott, my role models. Because of you, I'm instilled with the spirit of entrepreneurship.

To my friend Pam Noda, the editor of this book. Because of you, I'm able to share what I've learned over the years.

To Business Network International (Rendezvous Chapter), my professional networking organization. Because of you, I've become the biggest fish in my local pond.

And finally, to the many clients, colleagues and friends who continue to see the value of sales coaching and sales training. My wish for you is to find the SOHO solution!

One Cold Day in Canada

It was my first day on the job as a licensed sales representative of CST Consultants Inc., exclusive distributor of the Canadian Scholarship Trust Plan. CST Consultants Inc. is the oldest and largest provider of registered education savings plans (RESP) in Canada. I was on my way to an appointment with a young couple interested in setting up an RESP to begin saving for their newborn's post-secondary education.

This was a typically cold winter day in Montreal, Quebec, Canada. It was about minus thirty degrees Celsius with the wind chill—so cold that your eyes start watering and your tears turn to ice. For appearance sake, I decided against wearing a parka, scarf and hat and opted to wear a nice suit and dress shoes instead. I ran from the heated taxi to the couple's front door and rang the doorbell.

There was no answer. After a few more attempts (and some aggressive knocking), I called the wife from my mobile phone. "Hello?" she answered. "Hello. It's Tom Abbott from CST Consultants. I believe we have an appointment today," I said. "Oh, I'm sorry, Tom, was that today?" she replied. "Yes, in fact I'm at your home (standing outside in the cold!) now," I said.

"Oh, I'm sorry, Tom. Could we reschedule for another day and time?" she asked. I agreed—and never heard from her again.

The following week, I attended my first sales team meeting and was afraid that it might be my last. Fortunately, my sales manager, Claude Gauthier, encouraged me to stick around and learn from the more experienced sales representatives. The person at the top of the sales tracking board was a woman named Gene. She possessed the two ideal qualities of high performance sales professionals: she was great with people and great with processes. Gene was able to qualify leads effectively, establish rapport with prospects quickly, determine their needs accurately and close sales confidently.

With nothing to lose, I asked Gene if she would be willing to share a few strategies to help me get my foot in the door with prospects and close sales. She agreed. After a few months of implementing those strategies, I went on to have a 100 percent closing ratio with zero policy cancellations!

Several years later, after leaving CST Consultants Inc. and moving from Montreal, Quebec, to Vancouver, British Columbia, I received a telephone call from the Head Office of CST Consultants Inc. They wanted my new mailing address because they had a cheque for me. I was reminded that they withheld 20 percent of our commissions and deposited them in a contingency fund to be refunded to customers who cancelled their policies. Because I had zero policy cancellations over several years, that amounted to quite a nice bonus.

The lesson I learned that one cold day in Canada was that my key to success would require a willingness to ask questions when I was struggling. The key to my success would require an essential quality and my first piece of advice for you:

BE CURIOUS.

Getting Started

You would probably agree that having a great product or service does not guarantee sales. If you have a terrific offering and are still struggling with sales, it's time to take a look at your selling strategy. Maybe your "selling strategy" consists of passively waiting for customers to visit your place of business or your website. By applying the strategies in this book, you'll begin taking a more proactive approach to growing your business. That way, you won't be leaving the success of your business to chance.

What Can Be Measured Can Be Improved

The first step in taking control of your sales is to identify how comprehensive your sales and marketing strategy is right now. What are you doing consistently and what are you not doing so consistently? You have to recognize where you are today in order to see where you're going and how to get there.

The following self-assessment tool makes the process a little easier by providing some structure. In the short exercise below, identify your strengths and weaknesses as honestly as possible. Ask a colleague, partner, or sales coach for their assessment of you as well.

The SOHO Solution Self-Assessment

For each statement, rate yourself 1 to 5 (1 = completely disagree; 5 = completely agree).

_____ 1. I have accurately discovered my niche.
_____ 2. I have created a list of qualifying questions.
_____ 3. I have had conversations with prospects to discover their greatest challenges.
_____ 4. I understand how the decision-making process and buying criteria differs between business-to-consumer and business-to-business customers.
_____ 5. I have discovered the top three ways of consistently reaching a large number of my ideal target customers.
_____ 6. I have a tool for organizing prospecting information.
_____ 7. I am totally familiar with the products I sell and can clearly communicate the features and benefits.
_____ 8. I have studied competitors to determine their advantages and disadvantages.
_____ 9. I have discovered what sets me apart from other solution providers.
_____ 10. I have identified the top three reasons why my ideal customer should choose me.
_____ 11. I have created a list of frequently asked questions.
_____ 12. I have compiled a compelling script for scheduling appointments.
_____ 13. I have created an assessment to accurately understand my prospects' needs.
_____ 14. I have established three ways to communicate with prospects that effectively engage them to take action.

____ 15. I am able to make compelling demonstrations of my product including proof devices.

____ 16. I have chosen my top three closing techniques, as well as a list of common objections and my responses to those objections.

____ 17. I focus on the future and how to improve rather than focusing on past mistakes and failures.

____ 18. I have a positive attitude as opposed to a negative attitude because I know that my attitude becomes a self-fulfilling prophecy.

____ 19. I am developing my "expert power" by engaging in personal and/or professional development activities.

____ 20. I am improving my communication style, manners, voice quality and non-verbal communication.

____ 21. I am establishing, building and maintaining strong relationships with key groups (partners, support staff, customers and secondary decision makers).

Total Score: ________

Scoring

101–105 Master Salesperson

You're either a sales guru or in complete denial! If it's the former, you're obviously a master of selling. If it's the latter, take the self-assessment again with your coach this time. Your biggest obstacle is likely yourself, so staying focused and motivated will be your greatest challenge. This book will help you stay on top of your game by revisiting sales and marketing fundamentals that sometimes get overlooked.

81–100 Strong

Congratulations! Clearly, you know how to sell. You're a natural and in some cases it just seems so easy! Your sales skills are habits and you seem to perform them automatically and without conscious effort. You are most likely skilled enough to close almost every sale. Your greatest challenge is being consistent in your sales and marketing efforts. Your drive to succeed will have you absorbing this book and consistently applying strategies to further improve the return on your sales and marketing investment.

61–80 Above Average

You're doing most things right and you're likely closing more sales than you're losing. You tend to put most learning into practice and are fairly confident when it comes to sales. However, you're much stronger in some areas than others and some things are falling through the cracks. Your greatest challenge is developing a more well-rounded strategy around sales. This book will help you concentrate on the specific areas that need attention, so your sales function becomes more automatic.

41–60 Average

The good news is you're probably doing some things right when it comes to sales and marketing. The bad news is you've discovered that about half of the businesses out there are much more competent than you are. You know that there are many things that you don't know, so your greatest challenge is raising your game in all areas. This book will raise your competency in sales and marketing, one strategy at a time.

21–40 Below Average

Success in sales requires a systematic approach, not luck. At the moment, you may have a complete lack of knowledge of the importance of sales and marketing fundamentals. You may not realize that there are many things you don't know, so your greatest challenge will be increasing your awareness. This book will help you become aware of the skills required to succeed in sales. If you're ready to reach more prospects and close more sales, you've bought the right book.

0–20 Weak

I'm glad you're reading this book. Your biggest obstacle is likely yourself, so your challenges will be keeping an open mind and staying willing to learn (and try) new things. Keep reading!

What the Numbers Mean

Every statement in the assessment will be addressed in this book. So completing the self-assessment will help you get the most out of The SOHO Solution. The self-assessment will help you identify your greatest learning opportunities and this book will help you improve your selling skills in those areas. Before you know it, you'll begin attracting your ideal target customer, differentiating yourself in the marketplace and converting more leads into sales.

What was your score? Before you start working with the weekly strategies, it's important to reflect on what the numbers mean for you. Keep in mind that the self-assessment is simply a road map showing where you are right now and what you need to do to reach your destination. Keep monitoring your progress by taking this self-assessment again a few months from now; the score will probably be very different. Different areas of your sales and marketing strategy will require your attention at different times. By reading the rest of this book and implementing the weekly sales strategies, you could become a master salesperson in less than six months!

Customer Fundamentals

1

Week 1 Strategy

Discovering Your Niche

Have you discovered your ideal target customer? As much as you might want to believe your product or service will benefit everyone, the truth is, not everyone feels the same way you do. Have you heard the expression "Jack-of-all-trades, master of none"? Most businesses tend to fall short because they try to be all things to all people.

Multinational corporations realize this and spend countless hours (and dollars) discovering their ideal target customer. They realize that while some products have mass appeal, others may appeal only to a relatively small segment of the market. Therefore, your first challenge is to discover your niche. Don't worry about excluding markets. Discovering your niche is about finding customers suited to your purpose, expertise and market trends.

Purpose

The first step in detecting your niche is to consider which market best fits your life purpose. When brainstorming possible markets, it's important to consider your level of "aliveness", how a market fits with your values, interests and personality, as well as the impact you feel you could have on that market. On a scale of one to five, with one being "not at all" and five being "absolutely", ask yourself the following questions:

1. How passionate am I about this market?
2. How in line is this industry with my values?
3. Am I genuinely interested in this market?
4. Does this industry allow me to be authentic?
5. How great an impact could I have on this market?

There are no wrong answers here. You're simply trying to discover which market best fits your purpose. Why is this so important? Because running your own business and being a sales professional can be very challenging at times. If you can discover a market that best fits your life purpose, you're more likely to stick with it during the difficult times.

Expertise

The second area to consider when identifying your ideal target customer is your expertise. It's important to think about your God-given talents, knowledge and skill, training, accomplishments and how easily you could position yourself as an expert. On a scale of one to five with one being "not at all" and five being "absolutely", ask yourself the following questions:

1. Could my God-given talents and natural gifts serve this market?
2. Would my life experiences resonate with this market?
3. Could my training benefit this industry?
4. Would my accomplishments resonate with this market?
5. Could I easily position myself as an expert?

At the end of the day, you need to position yourself as an expert in your field. Customers want you to have experience, training and accomplishments helping people like themselves. More and more, customers are looking for specialists, not generalists. If you're able to confidently answer YES to the questions above, you're on your way to establishing yourself as an expert in that field.

> "Have you heard the expression "Jack-of-all-trades, master of none"? Most businesses tend to fall short because they try to be all things to all people."

Trends

The third area to pay attention to is trends in the market. It's important to consider your ideal target customers' greatest challenges and their ability to pay. You should also note the amount of competition, the size of the market and how easy it would be to reach your ideal customers. On a scale of one to five, with one being "not at all" and five being "absolutely", ask yourself the following questions:

1. Is this market actively seeking solutions to their problems?
2. Does this industry have the ability to afford my services?
3. Is this an under-served segment of the market?
4. Are there enough customers to sustain my business?
5. Can I easily reach these customers?

Some preliminary research will give you a very good indication of the trends in the market. Finding an under-served segment of the market that is still large enough to sustain your business is important. Identifying ways to easily reach these customers (see week 4) through traditional and new media will be critical to your success.

Week 1 Action

Your task this week is to answer in writing each of the questions in this chapter. They'll provide the foundation for discovering your niche and identifying your ideal target customer. Going through this exercise by considering your purpose, your expertise and the needs of the market for each possible niche should give you a good indication as to the top two or three markets that you may want to research further.

2

Week 2 Strategy

Qualifying Prospects

Identifying people as prospects (prospecting) is a very important aspect of personal selling. You qualify prospects by asking three questions.

1. Do they have a need for your product?
2. Do they have the ability to pay for your product?
3. Do they have the authority to purchase your product?

Always keep these three questions in mind and keep refining your prospect list to help you avoid wasting time calling on people who are unlikely to do business with you.

To help you accurately qualify your prospects and make sure you are speaking to the right people, you need to create a list of qualifying questions. For example, in the case of an immigration consultant, a good qualifying question might be, "Are you planning on moving to a new country?" The important word in that question is "planning". If the person answers that they are not planning on moving to a new country, they might just be curious and are probably not a serious prospect.

Ask Specific Questions

The immigration consultant could further qualify prospects by asking when they are planning on moving. Are they planning on moving within the next week, the next month, within three months, six months, a year or more? Answers to specific questions like these give you a very good indication of how qualified a prospect is.

You also want to qualify prospects by determining whether they can afford your product or service. Again, in the case of an immigration consultant, it might be useful to let prospects know that immigrating to a new country typically costs between x and y amount and then ask them if they could afford that amount right now. If they can't afford that amount right now, then they clearly cannot afford your services and are not in a position to move forward.

> "Keep refining your prospect list to help you avoid wasting time calling on people who are unlikely to do business with you."

It's also useful to ask prospects the following question: "Who else needs to be included in this decision?" You want to be sure that you're speaking with the right person—that is, someone who actually has the authority to make the buying decision. In the case of an IT services provider, for example, you could ask: "Who else should be involved in this meeting?" The answer to this question will clearly indicate who the real decision maker is and will ensure that you're not wasting your time speaking to the wrong person.

Asking these types of qualifying questions during your initial contact (and regularly throughout the sales process) with prospects will help you determine right away whether someone is in fact a qualified prospect. To increase sales, you must increase the quantity and quality of prospects. You can shorten the sales cycle by properly qualifying prospects.

Week 2 Action

Your task this week is to create at least three qualifying questions. Going through this exercise will help you identify your ideal target customers. Prospects' answers to these questions will help ensure that you are talking to the people most likely to do business with you.

Week 3 Strategy

Having Conversations with Prospects

3

It's common for business owners to develop products and services that they are certain will appeal to their customers. The only problem is that many times they haven't asked their customers first! Before investing any more time and money promoting products that you love, find out what your customers love. Your answers to the questions for week 1 should give you a good indication as to the top two or three markets that you may want to research further.

This week, we'll focus on having conversations with prospects to clarify their needs. You can do that by scheduling twenty-minute meetings with your prospects to ask them the following questions:

1. What are the greatest challenges you face?
2. Are you overcoming those challenges now?
3. How are you trying to overcome those challenges?
4. Are you satisfied with how my competitors are servicing you?
5. What other solutions are you looking for?

Fact-Finding Mission

The purpose of these meetings is to uncover your prospects' greatest challenges and what they're doing now, if anything, to overcome those challenges. You're on a fact-finding mission and the answers to these questions will help you see if you can match your solution to their challenges. This will also allow you to modify your offering if necessary. Avoid the temptation to start selling.

Pick up the phone or send an email to at least three people within each of the three markets you want to research further. What you'll find is that one or two of those markets are easier to reach than others. This can give you a very good indication of how challenging it might be to offer your products and services to a particular market.

"You're on a fact-finding mission and the answers to these questions will help you see if you can match your solution to their challenges."

If, for example, you're having difficulty scheduling a meeting with someone within a certain industry simply to learn about their challenges, imagine how difficult it is going to be for you to actually try to get in front of them to make a sales presentation. If, however, you find that for one particular market all of your calls are answered, your emails are returned and appointments are scheduled, that's a very encouraging sign.

Don't be discouraged if prospects are already doing business with someone else. In fact, this is a good sign. It means they're already spending money trying to find solutions to their challenges. That is a good prospect. They don't need to be convinced of the need to solve this problem because they're already trying to solve it. You'll simply need to demonstrate how you are the ideal solution provider.

If prospects are already doing business with someone else, ask them the following questions:

1. What is it about them that you like?
2. How are they meeting your needs?
3. What are they doing well? And not so well?

The answers to these questions will help you learn what your market needs and what satisfies them. But you won't know that until you have these conversations with them. Take notes. This is market research. No one knows what your customers want more than your customers themselves. Save yourself time and money when developing products and services by getting it right the first time.

Week 3 Action

Your task this week is to schedule twenty-minute meetings with three people within each of the markets you want to research further. Be sure to ask them each of the questions listed in this chapter. The answers to these questions will help you develop products and services based on what your market needs and finds satisfying.

Week 4 Strategy

Understanding the Decision-Making Process

4

Are you selling to businesses or consumers? If you don't think it makes a difference, think again. You bought this book to learn how to sell, but it's more important for you to learn how and why customers buy.

The decision-making process and buying criteria differs between business-to-business (B2B) and business-to-consumer (B2C) customers. These differences can help you determine which market you might want to serve. Here are some common steps in the buying process:

1. Recognizing that something is wrong, imperfect, or incomplete.
2. Searching for information and evaluating available alternatives.
3. Making a decision to do something.

Selling to Businesses

The B2B market can be segmented into five different markets: other businesses, governments, educational institutions, wholesalers and retailers. I've noticed a trend towards business services, particularly those which help companies increase productivity and profitability through innovation processes and technology (often web-based).

When selling to businesses, make sure you have a functional (not simply fashionable) website and an email address ending in @yourcompany.com. Nothing says amateur more than you@gmail.com! If your website is still a "work in progress", consider creating a business page on Facebook. The page is free and has most of the features you'd likely have with a website. And since it's on the Facebook platform, you can gain legions of fans to "like" your business more quickly than with your website.

> "You bought this book to learn how to sell, but it's more important for you to learn how and why customers buy."

There are naturally fewer B2B customers than there are B2C customers, but businesses have tremendous buying power. This means that you don't need to have as many B2B customers to sell the same volume as you would need with B2C customers. Business customers tend to be concentrated within a certain geographic area (for example, central business districts or industrial trade parks), but communication and technology have in many ways made the saying "location, location, location" obsolete.

Companies typically have a formal buying process and much time is spent evaluating alternatives because the dollar value of purchase can be very high. It can sometimes take a considerable amount of time locating a decision maker in an organization. Just when you think you're speaking to the right person, you discover that in fact he or she is not the decision maker. You might even find that in some cases there are several stakeholders who will all be involved in the buying decision. For example, the CEO who is interested in return on investment, a general manager who is interested in staying on budget and a project manager who is interested in seamless integration for ease of use. Three different people with three very different needs.

Some companies will also perform a comprehensive vendor analysis to help them determine your ability to offer reliable fulfillment in the appropriate quality and quantity. Companies want to make sure you're able to deliver on time, on budget and in the quantities that they are seeking. Many companies are also using centralized purchasing systems for their locations. This helps them secure better pricing on volume purchases and could help you sell to multiple locations through one contact.

B2B selling involves developing long-term relationships. Companies are looking at ways to form partnerships that will help them mutually increase productivity and profitability. Business decisions are sometimes made in social settings like networking events, tennis courts and even food courts! Spending more time in face-to-face situations with customers is a great way to build relationships and build your business.

Selling to Consumers

There are naturally more consumers than businesses, but consumers purchase in much lower volume than organizations do. Therefore, in order to achieve your income goals, you would have to reach more consumer customers than you would business customers.

Studying consumer behaviour will help you understand why people buy certain products and allow you to react to trends in the marketplace. For example, people are spending less time at home and consuming entertainment and news on the go. iPhones and Kindles are in and DVDs and bookstores are out.

Let's look at me as an example of consumer behavior. Before making my decision to purchase a MacBook laptop recently, I went through each of the steps in the buying process. I recognized that something was wrong when the Keynote presentations I created on my Mac mini showed up in different formatting in PowerPoint on clients' PCs. I found a way to address the problem temporarily, but my solution wasn't convenient or comfortable.

I needed a laptop computer. The most important factors for me were quality and compatibility with my Mac mini. My research on the Internet led me to three alternatives: MacBook, MacBook Pro or MacBook Air. After further assessing the specifications of each laptop and their respective prices, I made a decision to purchase the MacBook. After deciding what to buy, I needed to decide from whom to buy.

While on business in Bangkok, Hong Kong and Jakarta, I would compare prices to those in Singapore. Hong Kong was the cheapest by a slight margin, but a colleague of mine in Singapore knew a shopkeeper in Funan Digital Mall who gave me an even better discount. For me in this situation, the buying process took some time, but I'm now the happy owner of a MacBook.

What Influences Buyers?

Having an understanding of Abraham Maslow's hierarchy of needs and theory of motivation could help you better understand what influences consumers. According to Maslow, individuals pass through five levels of needs:

- Physiological
- Security
- Social
- Esteem
- Self-actualization

For example, when consumers purchase food they're satisfying their physiological needs. Computer back-ups satisfy security needs. Networking events satisfy social needs. Awards satisfy esteem needs. Learning a new language satisfies self-actualization needs.

What consumer needs are being fulfilled by your product or service? You might find that there could be more prospects at the lower end of the scale (physiological), but you might also find a lot more competition. For example, if you're thinking of opening a restaurant because everybody needs food, you'll find no shortage of restaurants. That doesn't necessarily mean you won't be successful, but I suggest you revisit the action items from week 1 to make sure that the market is not saturated. At the higher levels of the hierarchy (self-actualization), there could be fewer prospects. But you might also find less competition, making that market slightly more attractive.

Week 4 Action

Your task this week is to determine (a) if you are selling to the right customers and (b) the manner in which customers are buying. Review the steps in the buying process described here. Understanding the decision-making process and buying criteria of your customers can help you shorten the sales cycle.

5

Week 5 Strategy

Discovering Ways to Reach Customers

It becomes much easier to develop a strategy to reach customers once you've finalized your market research. Success in sales requires discovering the top three ways of consistently reaching large numbers of your ideal target customer.

Why three ways? Well, to avoid putting all of your eggs in one basket with just one way and to avoid spreading yourself too thin in time and money with more than three ways. Sticking to your top three ways of consistently reaching a large number of your ideal target customer is manageable and will keep you focused.

Why the word "consistently"? Because anything other than being consistent doesn't work. If you're thinking that you can hit the jackpot with one full-page advertisement in a newspaper or magazine, you need to think again. Spending thousands of dollars on that type of strategy will almost guarantee you a negative return on your investment. And there's nothing less effective than attending a networking event, making some good contacts and not returning the following month and the month after that. Your audience needs to see you as consistent

> "Sticking to your top three ways of consistently reaching a large number of your ideal target customer is manageable and will keep you focused."

and credible before trusting your message.

Why the words "large number"? Because you'll need to reach lots of prospects in order to achieve your income goals and make the best use of your time. Joining your prospects' industry association could give you access to hundreds, if not thousands, of your ideal target customer. You could speak at their events, write articles for their publications, volunteer on committees. Consider using Facebook and publishing a blog or a newsletter as ways of reaching customers in large number.

Some ways to reach prospects include:

- Getting referrals.
- Speaking engagements.
- Networking events.
- Trade shows.
- Search engine optimization.
- Search engine marketing.
- Contacts within your center of influence.
- Online and offline directories or publications.
- Submitting articles to publications and websites.
- Writing a newsletter or blog.

- Using Facebook, Twitter, LinkedIn.
- Being interviewed on radio and television (you could also call in!).
- Advertising.
- Cold calling / cold emailing.

Cold Calling

If you're going to make cold calls, you need to be consistent with that strategy and make a LOT of calls. It could take ten calls to qualified prospects to get one customer. That's ten calls to people who are looking for your product or service, have the ability to pay for it and are in a position to make the buying decision.

Because not all prospects will be high quality, there's a good chance that you'll need to call one hundred people in order to land one sale! That's why I put cold calling and cold emailing at the bottom of the list. It's better to have people calling you, than the other way around. You'll probably close more than 90 percent of those in-bound calls and less than 10 percent of your out-bound cold calls. Where do you think it makes more sense to focus most of your attention? In week 12, I'll teach you how to craft compelling scripts for those times when you do want to make cold calls.

Measuring Results

With these top three things you're doing to reach your ideal target customer, be sure to measure the results. Keep track of how many calls you made last week. Look at how many appointments you scheduled compared with how many prospecting calls you made. Look at the number of appointments made divided by the number of sales made. Look at the number of calls made and the amount of time it took you to make those calls. Look at the dollar amount in sales divided by the number of hours it took to make those sales. Measure your results every step of the way. In week 17, I'll teach you how to break down your goals into daily activities.

The same can be done with search engine marketing. Look at how many hits you're getting on your website. Compare that with how many inquiries you're getting. Compare that with how many presentations you're delivering. Compare that with how many sales you're making. By making these comparisons, you can see which are the most effective ways of getting customers. What should you be doing more of? What should you be doing less of?

Look at the return on investment for networking events, trade shows, public speaking, or advertising in newspapers or magazines. Evaluate how worthwhile the impressions that you made were. How many times did you gain exposure? How much did each form of exposure cost you? How many inquiries did you get as a result? How many presentations came out of those inquiries? How many sales came from those presentations?

Tracking allows you to measure the effectiveness of each of your prospecting activities. This goes back to having conversations with prospects to get a deeper understanding of what they're looking for. Use tools like Google Insights and Google Analytics to get a deeper understanding of what your target customer is searching for (pay particular attention to the keywords they use for finding solution providers in your field online) and how they are behaving on your website. Make sure you can be found when they're looking for you.

There's no shortage of things that you can do to get in front of your ideal target customer. You just need to make a commitment to go after that group 100 percent using your top three ways of reaching them.

Week 5 Action

Your task this week is to identify the top three ways of reaching a large number of your ideal target customer. Review the sources of prospects identified in this chapter and decide which three would be most effective. Keep track of your time spent on prospecting activities and measure your results.

Week 6 Strategy

6

Organizing Prospecting Information

Now that you've found the top three ways of consistently reaching a large number of your ideal target customer, you're going to start getting more and more inquiries. So how are you going to organize all of your contact and payment information?

Using a database or a customer relationship management (CRM) tool will help you store and record this information systematically. You can use this tool to record how prospects heard about you, to help determine when you should follow up with prospects and existing customers and to help you remember what you and a customer talked about during your last conversation or when you should invoice your customer.

Take some time to think about what kind of information you want to keep track of. The date of your last contact with a customer? The date of the next contact? The date expected to close? Is there any supporting material you should be sending them? What are the names of the other stakeholders who will be involved in the buying decision? Any other special notes or comments? You can customize your CRM tool to track whatever information you choose.

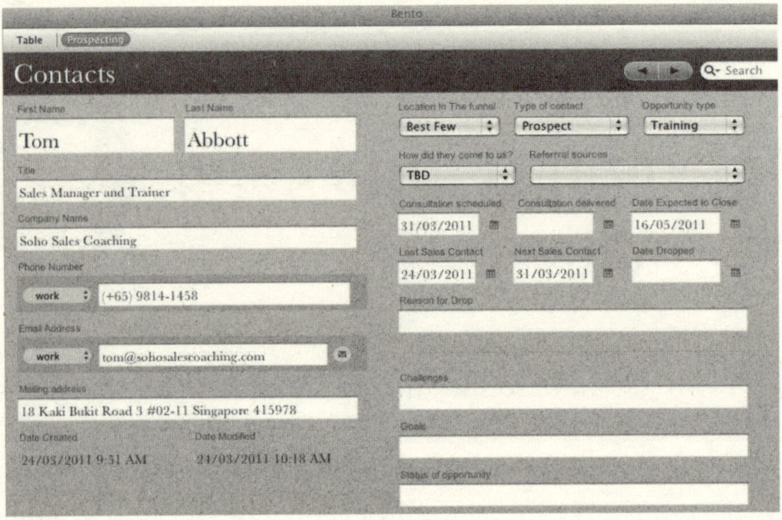

Know Your Customers

A lasting business relationship is based on a strong personal relationship between you and your customer. Learn the correct pronunciation and spelling of their name. Know their age. Become familiar with their experience, educational background, family status and special interests and hobbies.

Be sure to collect business-related facts as well. What does the company manufacture? How long has the company been in business? Is it a leader in its industry? Does it have plans to expand? You need to know your customers inside and out.

Show Me the Money

It's also useful to develop a prospecting and sales forecasting plan. A major barrier regarding prospecting is time. But because prospecting is so important to your long-term success as a business owner and as a sales professional, you need to take the time to develop an organized approach to prospecting. Prepare a list of prospects and forecast the potential sales volume that might be generated by each new account for each product. Just seeing those numbers on paper can be so motivating when you realize that one phone call could be worth thousands of dollars! Next allot a certain time period for contacting prospects (and customers too) for a visit. Schedule each prospect that agrees to meet with you into the time period that you have slated for such appointments.

Following Up

There is nothing worse than scribbling important information on sticky notes and losing them later. There goes the contact information or other details about prospects whom you met at networking events or trade shows, or who telephoned you direct. Now you don't know when to follow up with what, or where to deliver

> "Prepare a list of prospects and forecast the potential sales volume that might be generated by each new account for each product."

to prospects what you promised them. Wouldn't it be better for you to have a process whereby when people called, you could use a tool on your computer to enter their contact information and any reminders to yourself?

CRM Tools

Bento by Filemaker, GoldMine, Landslide, Microsoft Access, Microsoft Dynamics CRM, Netsuite, Outlook, PipelineDeals, Sage ACT!, Salesforce.com, Sales Logix, Siebel, SAP, Sugar CRM and Zoho CRM are examples of CRM or sales force automation tools. There are many others. I'm using Bento and Constant Contact. Many of these tools offer a thirty-day free trial and give credits for referring new customers. You have nothing to lose and everything to gain. Be sure to do your research by trying an online demonstration or downloading a trial version.

Don't spend too much time researching. Come up with a list of two or three CRM tools. Test them out for about a week to see which tool you'd be comfortable using on a regular basis. Then make a decision to move ahead. Start developing a process for organizing your prospecting information today. With practice, using it will become a habit.

Week 6 Action

Your task this week is to research two or three CRM tools and start testing them out. Once you've made a decision to start using the tool on a regular basis, it will be much easier to follow up with customers and prospects.

Product Fundamentals

Week 7 Strategy

Becoming Familiar with Your Products

7

There's good news and bad news. I'll start with the bad news: Buyers have more choices available to them now than ever before and that complicates the buying process. Now, the good news: Becoming a product expert will simplify and shorten the buying process for your customers.

Customers want to know how your product is tested, modified and retested. Performance data and specifications are important to most prospects. They also often want information about maintenance and service contracts. You should be able to supply accurate price and delivery information about your products and those of your competitors.

The more complex and expensive your products are, the more you're likely to get a favorable response, especially in B2B selling, if your proposal demonstrates increased productivity and profitability. Rather than saying how much a product costs, try talking about how your product can help them get more done in less time. Or talk about how your product can help them earn more money.

You Are the Product

In the eyes of your customer, you represent the business and they expect you to be knowledgeable. They'll want to know more about you as a person. What's your background? What do you bring to the table? What's your story? You are the one with whom customers will expect to share the history and mission of your organization. What's your company's brand story? (We'll talk more about that in week 9 and week 10 .) So be prepared.

With so many choices available to customers today, quite often a decision to buy will come down to the relationship that a customer has with you. Once a customer does buy, be sure to keep in touch by providing after-sales service.

Features and Benefits

Features answer the question, What is it? Benefits answer the question, What's in it for me? People don't buy features, they buy benefits. Focus on benefits that directly relate to specific buyer needs. Try using bridge statements to connect a statement of features with a statement of benefits. For example, "This hybrid vehicle runs on gasoline and electricity [feature], which means [bridge] you'll cut your fuel bills in half [benefit]."

One of my clients struggled with this very issue. As a digital signage solution provider, he had a really cool technological product, but he struggled describing the features—and more importantly, the benefits—to his customers. He found himself using technical language like resolution, pixels, dots-per-inch, servers and VGA over CAT5 Extender Sets! Customers are less interested in all the bells and whistles than they are in how a product can improve their lives. My client's customers were more interested in how they could use these screens to promote their products and services to their customers within their stores. That's the benefit they really wanted. That's all they cared about. So I helped my client make presentations that spoke his customers' language. Here's an example: "We're a local business helping retailers use screens in their stores to display their latest promotions and much more with customers. We're helping businesses such as yours and we can help you too. Contact us today for a free consultation and demonstration."

> "People don't buy features, they buy benefits. Features answer the question, What is it? Benefits answer the question, What's in it for me?"

Product Knowledge

The importance of having solid product knowledge cannot be overstated. Again, customers want to know how your product is tested, modified and retested. They want performance data and specifications. Customers are looking to you as being the product expert. What I'm saying is, they don't necessarily want you to train them to become product experts. They assume that you already are the expert. So be sure to do your homework so that you can answer any questions they have.

As I said before, people don't buy features, they buy benefits. So practice explaining the benefits of a product's features. What I mean is, select a feature and then talk about why that feature is important to the customer. That's your bridge statement. Using bridge statements helps you transition from features to benefits and demonstrates that you understand how your customer wants to benefit from your product.

Here's another example, with the feature statements and benefit statements indicated: "We offer 42- inch display screens [feature] so that [bridge] your customers can see your message anywhere in the store [benefit]. We use wired connections instead of cellular connections to display your content [feature], which means [bridge] you never have to worry about losing the connection [benefit]. You can try our service free for 30 days [feature] so that [bridge] you can make sure it works before buying it [benefit]."

Many of my clients have noticed that customers are looking more and more for customized solutions, as opposed to off-the-shelf generic solutions. With so many solution providers offering similar products and services, becoming a product expert should be one of your priority goals. Customers are full of information, but they are starving for knowledge. One of the best ways you can assist customers is by helping them make sense of all the information that's available to them. In fact, these days most customers are well informed about product specifications and features. Your job is to help them make sense of this information by helping them understand what it means to them.

When you're dealing with complex sales, you need to pay particular attention to product configuration. This means selecting the right products and services for your customer. In the case of the digital signage provider, he often has to customize a solution by bringing together many components of his company's overall product mix-whether it be LCD or Plasma screens or servers and other high-tech equipment.

Written Proposals

When you're selling to organizations, you'll frequently need to include written proposals in your overall product strategy. This is where you lay out your specific game plan for helping your customer. Done well, your written proposal can actually set you apart from the competition because it allows your customer to see everything laid out in detail: the features, the benefits and the value that you will be adding.

When writing proposals for organizations, outline the long-term objective the company is looking to achieve and the key medium- and short-term goals they are hoping to accomplish as a result of your product or service. Then present the solution that you will be offering them to help them reach their goals. This solution lays out in detail the solution you will deliver, the duration and the company's investment. Also include supporting information outlining the benefits to their organization, how you have helped companies like theirs in the past, what clients say about your business, a brief biography and examples of media exposure.

When selling to organizations, it often comes down to their return on investment. Companies need to justify the financial reasons to buy. They need to make a business case to buy. So if you can demonstrate to your business customers through your sales proposal how they will get a healthy return on their investment, you will more likely get a favorable response.

Become a Product Expert

So how do you become a product expert? Start by reading your product literature. Read your brochures, pamphlets, catalogs and advertisements. Go on a plant tour to see firsthand how your products are produced. Not only will this enhance your product knowledge, it will also help increase your enthusiasm for the products you sell because you'll have seen them being made firsthand. Talk to other people in your organization: salespeople or customer service people or delivery people. Learn from them. Talk to your customers. Who knows more about your products and services than your customers? They've seen your product firsthand under normal working conditions, in everyday situations. Your customers can give you a realistic assessment of the strengths and weaknesses of your products or services. Listen to them. Have you tried your own products or service? Using your products and services and carefully evaluating them will improve your product knowledge and confidence.

One final word of caution. Now that you're a product expert, resist the temptation to share all your knowledge with every customer that walks in the door. You need to know everything about your products and services, but your customer doesn't. Keep the conversation focused on the benefits they receive by purchasing your product and how your product helps them. At the end of the day, people care about what's in it for them.

Week 7 Action

Your task this week is to become a product expert. Read your product literature, see how your product is produced, speak with colleagues and customers. This will make you a more valuable resource for your customers.

Week 8 Strategy

Studying Companies that Sell Similar Products

8

It's important to study companies that sell products similar to yours so that you can determine if they have a competitive advantage or disadvantage. Your competition is helping you do this and they don't even know it.

Perhaps you're thinking, "What do you mean they're helping me? They're trying to put me out of business!" Well, here's some good news. Your competitors are posting information on their websites about their history, products, services, terms and conditions, delivery information, price packages, frequently asked questions—and sometimes even their suppliers or partners. This information is readily available, displayed for the world to see. Your competitors are doing this to try to inform their customers. But this information is available to you as well.

Positioning Your Business

The information on a competitor's website helps you to see their competitive advantages and disadvantages. To help you learn from competitors, here are some questions worth asking:

- What do they do very well?
- What don't they do quite as well as you do?
- What are some areas where they're leading the industry?
- How are they positioning themselves?
- What is their brand?
- What are their strengths?
- What are their weaknesses?
- What areas are beyond their expertise?
- Are there opportunities for you to fill the gaps?

It can be very difficult to position yourself and determine how you're different or better than the competition if you don't even know what they're offering. Sometimes it can also be hard to decide how much you should be charging for products and services. So studying the competition provides a frame of reference. Your competition has a strong influence on your sales strategy. In fact, acquiring knowledge about your competitors can actually help develop and increase your overall product knowledge.

"Acquiring knowledge about your competitors can actually help develop and increase your overall product knowledge."

One of my clients was struggling to describe his products and services, so I suggested that he visit the websites of about three of his major competitors. I wanted him to take a look at their product offerings and their packages. After doing that, my client was able to see how easily his competitors communicated their offerings. He drew inspiration from their websites and discovered ways he could describe his own services. This exercise also gave him a great opportunity to see how he was better in some ways than the competition.

Another client of mine visited some of her competitors' websites and discovered they were charging a lot more than she did for delivering the same type of service. That helped her make a decision to increase her fees so that she could both be more credible in the marketplace and get a greater return on her investment.

Study the Competition

Prospects often ask about competing businesses. Your answers to those questions could help you sell your product or service. Your attitude toward the competition is important. Always avoid criticizing them because doing so will only make you look unprofessional. And make sure you get your facts straight so that you remain credible. Indeed, it's often best to avoid referring to the competition altogether. Keep the focus away from them and squarely on your business and how you can help. Provide value every step of the way when dealing with prospects by offering great service and additional information, knowledge, or consulting. This can often neutralize a competitor's proposal.

Here's what I suggest you do to study the competition. Start by doing an Internet search using keywords that your prospects would use to find solutions to their problems. There's a great online tool called Google Insights. Just type in certain keywords and it will display the current top search terms along with keywords that are rising in popularity as search terms on the Internet.

Once you have found your competition, visit the websites of five or ten of the most relevant search results and grab your pen and paper. Start noting areas of specialty, products and services offered, how those products and services are delivered, pricing and so on. What does your competition do better and differently than you? What do you do better and differently than your competition? Remember, only by studying your competitors can you determine if they have an advantage or disadvantage.

Week 8 Action

Your task this week is to study the competition. Visit the websites of your top competitors and take note of their offerings. This will provide a frame of reference for identifying your position in the market.

Week 9 Strategy

Discovering What Sets You Apart

9

In a world where buyers are inundated with choices, how can you stand out from other solution providers? To help differentiate yourself from the competition, here are some questions worth asking:

- Are you the oldest and largest business in your industry?
- Do you have the biggest selection available?
- Are you offering the lowest price guarantee?
- Do you guarantee the fastest delivery?
- Are you offering the hottest, newest products or services?

It all comes down to positioning. While there's no right or wrong answer, you do need to pick at least one of these categories in order for you to stand apart from your competition. If you're not among the top three within your chosen area of differentiation, you will get lost. Let's talk about each of these categories.

Established and New Brands

When I was a licensed representative of the Canadian scholarship trust plan, one of the things that was a great differentiator between us and the competition was that we were the oldest and largest provider of registered education savings plans (RESP) in Canada. We'd been helping families save for their children's post-secondary education since the 1960s. Which means, we had more experience helping parents save money than anybody else. Although the company had been around for more than forty years, I personally didn't have that much experience in the industry. But the strength of the organization's history was a strong selling point with customers.

You can go in the opposite direction. You could position your business as being the new kid on the block. We are innovative, we are cutting edge, we've got fresh new ideas, we're all about the change that you need. Again, you need to pick up a point of differentiation and go for it.

Mass and Niche Market Brands

Another way to differentiate yourself is by having the biggest selection available. I'm sure you know some mass retail stores that have adopted this differentiation strategy very well. Basically, whatever you're looking for, they've got it.

At the opposite end of the spectrum are companies that target a specific niche market. They specialize in offering a certain type of product or service. For example, Havaianas only sells flip flops[1]. They've got dozens if not hundreds of different kinds of flip flops in their stores and that's all they sell. They specialize in flip flops. So if you're looking for flip flops, they've got them.

Low-Priced Brands

Maybe you want to offer the guaranteed lowest price. This is certainly an option, although it's not one that I recommend for most businesses. What often ends up happening is that customers start seeing your products or services as a commodity with no real value. They end up negotiating your price down to nothing. Yet there might be situations where you are genuinely able to acquire your inventory from manufacturers and suppliers at a substantially lower price than your competitors acquire their inventory. Or perhaps you're able to eliminate intermediaries and can sell directly to the consumer at a much lower price than your competition can. So in cases like this, offering the lowest price guarantee could be a good way of differentiating your business.

Service Brands

One way of positioning your business is by offering the fastest delivery or fastest service. This means being quick to respond or having fast turnaround time. Look at a company like Federal Express. "When it absolutely, positively has to be there overnight." This slogan has differentiated their business. If you need it there fast, call FedEx. How about Domino's Pizza? Here's a company whose guarantee was delivering your pizza

---

1 In March 2011, they officially announced their first closed toe line.

in thirty minutes or less—or the pizza is free. Their business is created around the infrastructure and the systems to deliver a product. "The pizza delivery experts" are not trying to sell you a high-quality pizza, they're trying to sell you a quickly delivered pizza. It's not that the product is not important, it's how fast it's being delivered that is the selling point.

Innovative Brands

Another way to differentiate yourself is by offering the hottest and newest products and services. Products like the iPhone and the iPad certainly are not competing on price or selection. They are examples of how Apple is always trying to churn out the hottest and newest product. We see this as cool, new and fresh. Many musical artists project this same image. Madonna, especially, has done an amazing job of reinventing herself throughout her career. From virgin, to dominatrix, to country and western singer, to Zen Buddhist, to disco queen—the list goes on and on. The only thing predictable about Madonna is her unpredictability. And that's her brand. That's what her customers want.

> "When customers think of your business, what exactly are they thinking? If they're not thinking anything, you are in big trouble."

Positioning is all the decisions, activities and communication strategies that are directed toward trying to create and maintain your intended product concept in the customer's mind. When customers think of your business, what exactly are they thinking? If they're not thinking anything, you are in big trouble. If they're thinking something other than what you want them to be thinking, you've got some work to do. It all comes down to positioning.

Signature Strengths

One way to discover what sets you apart from other solution providers is to ask your customers why they picked you.

1. What do they see as your strengths?
2. Which of your qualities are most important to them in your work together?
3. What is most valuable to them in your work together?

You could also do an online questionnaire that measures character strengths, such as the one developed by Dr. Seligman, Director of the University of Pennsylvania Positive Psychology Center (http://www.authentichappiness.sas.upenn.edu). Pick your top three strengths and then use bridge statements to clearly communicate how your strengths benefit your customer. For example, in my case, I'm always exploring and discovering new tools (my strength) that can help clients increase their sales (the benefit to the customer).

In the end, figuring out how to differentiate yourself from other solution providers means asking yourself this: What do you want to be known for?

Week 9 Action

Your task this week is to discover your point of differentiation. Ask your current customers why they picked you and what they see as your strengths. This will help you focus on communicating what's truly important to your prospects.

Week 10 Strategy

Identifying Reasons to Choose Your Business

10

You've heard of the elevator speech. That's the scenario where as you're riding the elevator, someone asks what you do and you only have sixty seconds to make a good impression before one of you gets off the elevator. Truth be told, no one actually talks in elevators, but I'm sure you get the point.

Crafting Your Pitch

When you need to say what you do, it's great to have a short and punchy phrase that pays. For example, my phrase is: I help small business owners make big sales. What's your phrase that pays?

There are some essential elements of a good pitch. It needs to be concise and clear. You should be able to explain what you do in sixty seconds or less. Your pitch needs to be targeted. This means it should be directed at a specific market or audience. It should name whom you help. Lastly, a pitch needs to be powerful so that you can make an impact on people and get some results.

It's also useful for your pitch to tell a story. People like stories. And stories help to make it easier for people to understand how your product or service can help someone like them, because in telling the story you're actually demonstrating how you've helped that "someone like them" in the past.

One element of a perfect pitch is the hook. A hook is something that's irresistible, something that gets people's attention. It grabs them by the collar and has them wanting to learn more. They want to hear more, so they ask you to tell them more.

Here's an example of a pitch: "My name is Tom Abbott of Soho Sales Coaching and I help small business owners make BIG sales by coaching them one-on-one. I'm the author of the book The SOHO Solution: 21 Selling Strategies for Growing Your Small Business. Using my Soho Sales Fundamentals methodology, I've helped small businesses achieve a 300 percent increase in revenue within only six months."

Why Customers Choose You

To develop marketing materials such as your pitch and to have more meaningful conversations with prospects, it's important to identify the top three reasons your ideal customers should choose you. Start by making a list of your natural gifts, life experience, training and accomplishments. Anything that can help you position yourself as an expert in your field. Next list what sets you apart in any of the following areas:

- Price
- Quality
- Service
- Selection
- Exclusivity
- Innovation
- Methodology

Look over your lists and choose the top three reasons your ideal customer should choose you as their solution provider. Remember that products and services solve problems and that people will only buy a product or service if they believe it will help them solve a problem.

A word of caution about the tactic of using low prices to differentiate yourself. Most people believe that low price equals low quality. If you're not able to fully demonstrate the quality of your product, having a low price may cause your product to be misjudged. Typically, selling something for a low price also means you're offering less service. It seems, however, that most customers want excellent after-sales service. So you might find yourself investing time and money on low-yield customers (people who buy your low-cost product but then expect a high level of after-sales service). Recently, a colleague of mine reminded me of the old story about customers wanting everything cheap, fast and good. Ask them to choose two!

Exceeding Expectations

If you're in business, you need to be adding value every step of the way. Being a better-trained salesperson adds value. More reliable deliveries add value. Great after-sales service adds value. Constantly innovating your products and services also adds value. Adding value can help give your company a competitive edge. Customers want more than a generic product. They assume that your product will deliver on its promise. They're always looking for more value, something more than they expect.

> "It's not just about being better. It's about being different. There's enough out there for everyone. But you need to give people a reason to choose you."

What could you do to surprise your customer? What could you do to exceed their expectations? Helping your customers see solutions to problems beyond what they currently see is one way. Looking out for your customers' long-term interests is another way. You need to think about what your customers are looking for. Are they transactional buyers—for example, running into a corner store to buy a chocolate bar? Or are they more consultative buyers who expect you to make significant time investments to really understand their needs and problems? And then there are relationship buyers. For this type, you're invested in the long-term interests of your customer. It's not just about helping them now; it could be about helping them and those around them for years to come.

Points of Contact

You can help your customers choose you by paying attention to your points of contact with them. A useful exercise is to study two or three of your competitors by noticing these different points of contact: business card, email, invoices, telephone greeting, voice mail greeting, store front, website, newsletter, blog, free assessment, free consultation, audio or video products, training programs, public speaking, teleseminars, webinars, workshops, design, packaging. The list goes on and on. Once you've taken a good look at how your competition is handling their points of contact with customers, think about your own points of contact with your customers. What can you do to give your customers reason to choose you?

Branding Your Business

Giving customers reasons to choose you is branding. Here's another great branding exercise. Try answering the following questions:

1. Have you created a proprietary methodology or approach?
2. What do you do and how do you do it?
3. How do you look, act, feel and perform?
4. What is your franchise, system, process and way of do things?
5. What is your positioning statement?

For example, "Soho Sales Coaching. Helping small business owners make BIG sales." That's my brand promise.

Review your signature strengths that you pinpointed. They are your personal strengths that you display every day in your business. Next review the top three reasons you identified in this chapter that your ideal target customer should choose you. Think about how these things brand you, or make you different from everyone else.

It's not just about being better. It's about being different. There's enough out there for everyone. I truly believe that. But you need to give people a reason to choose you. If you're the same as everybody else, you get lost in the crowd. Answering the questions in this chapter will get you closer to defining your brand.

Week 10 Action

Your task this week is to discover reasons for customers to choose your business. Brainstorm the essential elements of what your business is about. This will help you craft the perfect pitch to use when speaking with prospects.

Week 11 Strategy

Compiling a List of Frequently Asked Questions

11

Because buyers have more choices available to them than ever before, they also seem to have more questions than ever before. Fortunately, you'll notice there are some questions that are asked more frequently than others. How does it work? How long does it take? How much does it cost? Take note of the questions that arise most often and rehearse your responses. This will help you anticipate and answer buyer concerns and objections during sales presentations.

Shorten the Sales Cycle

You can even have a list of frequently asked questions, along with your answers, posted on your website and included in other marketing materials. Doing this will help create a better-informed consumer, which could shorten the sales cycle. You won't have to spend so much time fielding the same basic questions from prospects. Wouldn't you prefer having customers call you who already know the answers to these questions and simply want to ask how quickly they can get started with you?

Rehearsing these questions and answers either on your own, with a colleague or a sales coach helps prepare you for situations when you are face to face with a prospect. This way you will be able to answer their questions comfortably and confidently. There's nothing worse than being caught by surprise with a question that you weren't prepared for. It feels even worse being hit with a question that you've heard a million times but for which you still haven't come up with a good answer. Again, customers are looking to you to be the expert.

Making Things Easier

I'm always surprised by how often prospects call businesses to ask questions and then don't buy. They seemed ready to buy because they felt compelled to take action by telephoning the company or sending an email. But once the business answers their basic information-gathering questions—How much does it cost? How does it work? What products do you have? How long does it take to get delivered? Does it come assembled?—the customer says thank you and is gone! Wouldn't it be better if customers already had the answers to those kinds of questions from your website beforehand? That way, when they contact you they'll be ready to place orders. This will make it a lot easier for you to convert prospects into paying customers.

Start by making a list of all of the questions that you have either heard customers ask or you can imagine them asking. Get a good list of five, ten, or twenty questions. Then think about your answers to those questions. What will you say? You could also try scheduling twenty-minute meetings with three of your prospects for the purpose of giving them an opportunity to ask all sorts of questions about your business. Remember to resist the temptation to sell; you're on a fact-finding mission. If you happen to sell some products and services, that's good too.

> "Wouldn't you prefer having customers call you who already know the answers to these questions and simply want to ask how quickly they can get started with you?"

Again, rehearse your answers so you become very comfortable and confident. Remember, sometimes prospects ask you questions not so much because they care about the answer, but because they want to know that you can answer the question. Customers want to feel as though they've done their job by asking the right questions. So you need to do your job by answering those questions well.

Week 11 Action

Your task this week is to compile a list of frequently asked questions. Make a list of five, ten, or twenty questions. Then formulate your answers to those questions. This will help you answer objections more confidently and close more sales.

Presentation Fundamentals

Week 12 Strategy

Creating Scripts for Scheduling Appointments

12

The idea is to create a compelling script for scheduling appointments that will resonate with your prospects. The most important thing to remember here is, Don't wing it!

It's so important to develop scripts for leaving messages on voice mail and with assistants (gatekeepers), as well as for when you are speaking directly with your prospects. Sometimes we feel as though we know our products and services so well that we can just pick up the telephone, make some calls and start talking. But the reality is that without some kind of a structure or plan, you leave too many things open to chance and can lose control of the call.

Purposes for Calling

Let's talk about the purpose of the call. This might seem obvious. I'm calling because I'm trying to get new customers, right? Well, in fact, you can have different purposes for calling prospects.

You could be calling prospects to inform them of something: you might say, "I just wanted to let you know that we're offering a free seminar next week, I thought it might interest you." Or you might say, "I'm calling to let you know that I saw an article in the paper last week that I thought you might be interested in. It's about something that affects your industry and I thought you might appreciate knowing what's going on." Here, in calling to simply inform a prospect of something, you can also help position yourself as an industry expert or as someone who cares. This way, you'll stay top of mind with them when they are looking for a solution provider such as yourself.

> "The reality is that without some kind of a structure or plan, you leave too many things open to chance and can lose control of the call."

Another purpose of your call could be to remind a prospect of something. Here you might be calling them simply to say, "I just want to remind you that we have an appointment next Thursday at 5:00 PM. I look forward to speaking with you then." You may also want to remind your prospects of a very important deadline. So, for example, if you are in tax preparation, you might want to remind prospects that the deadline for filing their income tax return is coming up within a couple of weeks. Notice how the objectives in these examples really have little to do with what we would consider selling. But those types of calls still put you top of mind with your prospect. Generally, those types of calls will be well received.

A third purpose of your call could be to persuade people. This is the type of call that you might associate more with selling. Here you try to persuade a prospect, or encourage them, or compel them to take an action or make a decision about something. This call objective is what we would typically associate with the kind of cold call where you're trying to schedule an appointment. Sometimes you might be trying to actually sell them something on the telephone right then and there. This kind of cold call isn't really my style, though it might be appropriate for some industries.

Introducing Yourself

Once you are crystal clear on your call objective, then it becomes easier for you to create the script that you're going to use when you're on the telephone. So let's talk about that now. Your telephone script has six different sections. The first section is your introduction, or the first few words you're going to say the moment your prospect picks up the phone.

Generally you would introduce yourself with, "Good morning, it's Tom Abbott calling from Soho Sales Coaching." Next most people would ask, "How are you today?" I'm not a big fan of this question. If you're genuinely asking me how I'm doing and if I'm giving you a genuine response, I could say, "I'm busy right now, I don't have time." Also, if you're asking this question and you really don't care how I'm doing, then you'll come across as insincere. I know that social norms dictate that we ask how someone is, but I wouldn't end the sentence with "How are you?" Rather, I would say, "Good morning, it's Tom Abbott calling from Soho Sales Coaching. How are you, have you got a minute?"

The question that I am genuinely sincere about asking and the one that I really want the person to answer honestly is, "Have you got a minute?" Or, "Do you have time to speak right now?" Or, "Is this a good time to speak?" Here you're controlling the call. There are only two possible answers to those questions. "Yes, this is a good time" gives you permission to continue with a script. "No, this is not a good time" gives you permission to ask them when would be a better time. Notice how you're controlling the call. If it's not a good time for them, ask them when would be a better time to call them back. Typically, people respond by asking, "What's it regarding?" Or, "What is this about?" Notice how the person has just given you permission to actually answer that question: now you can tell them right then and there why you're calling. No matter which way a person responds, you win when you introduce yourself.

Building Rapport

The second section of your script deals with building rapport. If you've had the good fortune to meet the person you're calling before, this is a great opportunity to actually say something like, "It was really nice meeting you at the last Chamber of Commerce event." If this is a completely cold call and you have never met this person before, you could say that their name appeared on a list of the leading businesses in your city. Here you're making use of a third party introduction, albeit rather loosely. You are also flattering the person a little bit by letting them know that you know of them because they are highly regarded by a reputable organization like the Chamber of Commerce, for example. Usually, a little bit of soft flattery will buy you a few extra seconds on the telephone.

Establishing Credibility

The third part of your script deals with who you are and why they should listen to you. This is where I would say, for example, "I am the author of the book The SOHO Solution: 21 Selling Strategies for Growing Your Small Business. I help small business owners make BIG sales through one-on-one sales coaching." So that lets them know who I am and how I help businesses like theirs.

Making Your Offer

The fourth section of your script deals with why you're really calling, what you're offering them and what you would like them to do. You need to remember that people are only interested in what's in it for them. They don't care how great your company is, how many customers you have, what you're doing, or what makes you special. They don't care about that unless you can frame it in the context of how it can help them. That's all they care about. You will have only a short period of time on the telephone, so what you say has got to make that impact quickly.

This is where I would typically say, "I'm calling to offer you a consultation—at no charge, of course—to help me learn more about your business and to quickly show you how I might be able to help you discover your ideal target customer, differentiate yourself in the marketplace and convert more leads into sales." Notice how I've thrown in some real benefit statements about calling you for your free consultation, during which you're going to learn how I can help you achieve three goals. Now if they're not interested in achieving those three goals, then you've done a good job of disqualifying them. Remember, it's a numbers game; you just move on.

I would then continue by saying, "I'm giving away these free consultations to people who I think would benefit and there's no pressure whatsoever. I'll only need thirty minutes of your time." Let the prospect know that there's no pressure and no obligation, that they have nothing to lose because the consultation is free and that they can only gain by speaking with you. Notice how I also was clear that I only need thirty minutes of their time. Something to note here is if you promise someone that you only need thirty minutes of their time during your presentation, you'd better be sure that you stick within the time limit. During your actual meeting, when you notice the time getting close to half an hour, ask for their permission to continue if they're interested. You want to be known as someone who under-promises and over-delivers, as opposed to being thought of as someone who over-promises and under-delivers.

Getting a Commitment

The fifth part of the script is referred to as the close, or better, the commitment. Here I ask the question, "Would you be interested in a free consultation?" Often people say yes. If they say yes, then you need to start narrowing down when the consultation will take place. Most rookies make the mistake of asking the customer, "What's a good time for you to meet?" And the answer typically is, "Well, I'm really busy this week and next week doesn't look good either, so can you call me back in three weeks?" That response helps nobody. You haven't done all this work on the call only to be blown off for another three weeks.

You need to ask the prospect leading questions that are closed-ended questions. For example, "Are Mondays, Wednesdays or Friday's better?" Ask them to commit to a day of the week. Then ask them, "Do mornings or afternoons work better for you?" Ask them to commit to a part of the day. Then narrow down the time. You could say, "How about Wednesday at 2:00 PM?"

Ending Your Call

The final part of your call deals with the conclusion. Here you need to thank the prospect for their time and let them know that you're looking forward to speaking with them again or meeting with them. Repeat the day and time of the appointment. It's important also to ask them to please call you if anything comes up between now and the date of the meeting. Provide them with your contact details so they can call you to reschedule, if necessary.

Something you must also do is to ask them, "How will this decision ultimately be made?" Repeat the question several times to find the true decision maker. Then ask, "How about we invite them to join our meeting?" These questions help you discover who is the actual decision maker in the organization and help make sure that you will be meeting with someone with the authority to make buying decisions.
One final note on scripts. Don't read your script while you're on the phone. The script is a guideline, a template. It's not something to be read word for word while you're speaking to

a prospect. Get to know your script by practicing in front of a mirror or rehearsing with colleagues or your sales coach, if you have one. Also, be sure to track the number of calls you make, the number of contacts you speak with, the number of appointments you schedule and so on. It's all about the numbers: what you can measure, you can improve. By following this strategy for creating telephone scripts, you're going to do a much better job of actually engaging prospects on your calls and booking more appointments.

Week 12 Action

Your task this week is to create a script for scheduling appointments that will resonate with prospects. Frame your remarks in the context of how a meeting with you will help them. This will make it easier to get in front of more prospects.

Week 13 Strategy

Creating a Needs Assessment

13

Many of us make the mistake of trying to sell our products or services before fully understanding our prospects' most pressing challenges. This is analogous to your doctor handing you a prescription before taking the time to fully understand your symptoms. Can you imagine that happening? Of course not. Following the same logic, then, you wouldn't promote your products and services to customers before you had a clear idea of what they need and what their problems really are.

Diagnose before Prescribing

You can carefully diagnose your prospects' symptoms by creating a needs assessment. The needs assessment is a checklist or diagnostic tool to use with your prospects. Just as a doctor would examine you before prescribing medicine for your cold or a mechanic would examine your car before estimating repair costs, you need to assess your prospects before selling to them.

The needs assessment is a benchmarking tool that compares your prospects' process, or how they're doing things now, to what you, as the expert, consider to be the industry standard or best practice. It provides a snapshot of the performance of a prospect's business and helps them to understand where they are in relation to a particular standard. And you set the standard. The assessment results often make the case for making changes in order to make improvements. That's where you come in.

When approached by prospects, go into that meeting prepared with a needs assessment. Have the needs assessment written down. Go through each question with the prospect and take note of their answers. Beginning with the end in mind allows you to prepare a written proposal based entirely on the answers to the needs assessment. So your proposal essentially is based on what they're stating they need. You're simply reflecting back to them that you're going to deliver what they're looking for.

Challenges and Solutions

You might be wondering what types of questions should appear on a needs assessment tool. Here's a great question to start with: What specific challenges are you facing? Simply ask this question, listen and take notes. People are more than happy to share with you what's not working and what their problems are. Because very few people even ask this question, you'll come across as a professional and as someone who genuinely cares about them.

Another question I find useful to ask as a follow-up is, "What have you tried to help overcome those challenges?" This helps to understand how motivated they are to find a solution to their problem. If they answer that they haven't tried anything yet or indicate that they've had the problem for a long time, this tells you that solving that problem is not a priority for them. Or, they may say that they've sent their team for training, they've had people come in to provide training, they've read books, they've done mentoring with their team—and still they are struggling with the same challenges. That tells you that they are motivated to solve this problem because they are trying everything and they're willing to invest time and money. And their willingness to invest time and money qualifies them as a prospect.

Next you want to ask your prospects what they have tried that worked. You know something must be working, so what is it? Give them credit for trying something and for the successes that they have achieved. The things that are working are pointers to what else you could incorporate in your solution—because, guess what, perhaps you could do what's been working better, faster, cheaper, or differently.

> "Beginning with the end in mind allows me to prepare a written proposal based entirely on the answers to the needs assessment."

I also find it useful to ask people about what didn't work. A good question is, What did you not like about that solution? Or, What do you think would have made it work better? These are really thought-provoking questions that help your prospects get their minds around how to better fix the problem and what their desired outcomes are. Their answers help you to start crafting the ideal solution for them.

Identifying Goals

Another important question to ask is, "What are your goals?" You'll find that some prospects are prepared to answer this question. They have a very clear sense of their goals and what they're hoping to accomplish. You'll find that other prospects have no clue. Your job here is to help them formulate and articulate their goals. Ask them questions about their goals for last year or what they achieved last year. Compare those responses with what they say they would like to accomplish this year.

The next few questions help you become more engaged with the prospect and help them see you as a partner. When you ask, for example, "What are you looking to achieve in our work together?", the prospect starts seeing you as part of the solution to their problem. They may respond with something like, "I see you coming in and addressing these three major issues." I also like asking, "What would success look like to you as a result of this solution?" And finally, "Looking back a year from now, what will need to have happened for you to know this has been successful?" This shows your prospect that you're not just in it for the quick buck, but that you're actually looking into the future and seeing what the outcome will look like down the road as a result of your work together. This is relationship and consultative selling, not transactional selling. This approach positions you as a long-term partner.

Focus on Your Approach

When creating your needs assessment, it is useful to start by taking a close look at your offering, your approach, your philosophy, your process. How do you do things? What's your system? My system, for example, is packaged as the Soho Sales Fundamentals methodology. Everything that I do is based on the twenty-one components included within that approach. My coaching is based on that approach, this book is based on that approach, my needs assessment is based on that approach.

Your needs assessment can be in the form of statements rather than questions. And each statement could be based on your approach. I ask my prospects, for example, to assess themselves in twenty-one different components of their sales strategy. These twenty-one components are benchmarks that I've developed over the past ten years.

Ask prospects to rate themselves on a scale of one to ten (1 = completely disagree; 10 = completely agree). Going through this self-assessment helps them both to create a snapshot of the performance of their business and to understand where they are in relation to the standards that you've set through your methodology.

Prospects can go through your assessment on their own or with you. I recommend sending the self-assessment to your prospects and asking them to complete it and return it to you prior to your appointment. This will allow you to customize your presentation and solution to specifically address their challenges.

A needs assessment is not only useful for determining the needs of prospects. It is also useful as a sales tool because it positions you as knowledgeable in your field and, ultimately, as the ideal solution provider. How many of your competitors are using either a self-assessment tool or needs assessment tool with their customers? Having this tool could be one of the ways you differentiate yourself from your competition and will better position you as the ideal solution provider.

Week 13 Action

Your task this week is to create a tool for identifying the needs of your prospects. Ask intelligent questions. This will better position you as the ideal solution provider.

Week 14 Strategy

Engaging Prospects Effectively

14

How do we define prospects? Prospects have three basic qualifications. First, they must have a need for your product—either a real need or a perceived need. Second, they must have the ability to afford your product. If someone says they don't have the budget or they have no income, they are not a prospect. Third, they must have the authority to purchase your product. You need to be speaking to people who meet these three criteria.

Different Kinds of Customers

Let's talk a little bit about different kinds of customers. New customers are consumers or businesses that have purchased your products or used your services for the first time. For whatever reason, these people have decided to give you a try. Some of these consumers or businesses will use your products and services only once. Others will become repeat customers who use you again and again. They are new clients. New clients are customers who have purchased your products or used your services a second or third time. These renewing customers become maturing clients when they have purchased your products or used your services for longer than three consecutive months.

There's no science to these definitions, but they sure help when you're analyzing your customer database. You need to treat these three types of customers very differently. Each type needs to be engaged to move through your sales funnel.

Prospects

How are you engaging your prospects, your new customers, your new clients and your maturing clients to move through your sales funnel? I have found that creating a newsletter and a blog and offering free consultations to qualified prospects are useful ways to motivate them to try my coaching services for the first time.

Let's talk about what you could put in a newsletter, for example. I typically include an update on what's going on at Soho Sales Coaching, upcoming events and sales tips useful to small businesses. What could you write about that would be of value or interest to your audience? I also like to include a testimonial or case study from a happy client that briefly describes what their business was like before they started working with me, how I was able to help them and what outcomes were achieved as a result of our work together. Testimonials are a great way of assuring prospects that you can help them find solutions to their problems.

It's nice to have a theme for your newsletter and I like to include a lead article that focuses on the theme. Because people like looking at photos and watching videos, including them in the lead article or another part of the newsletter is effective. They catch people's attention and show that you are active and have embraced technology.

Because people don't have a lot of time to read newsletters, I'll often run just the few paragraphs of the article followed by a link to the article on my website. This serves a couple of purposes. It allows your reader to take a look at the full article at a later time on your website, which increases the amount of traffic to your website. It also increases the likelihood that the reader will actually visit some other pages on your website. The more time someone spends on your website, the greater the chance that they'll become a paying customer.

There are many great tools out there that you can use to build an online newsletter. You don't have to be a technological wizard anymore. You could try signing up for a free trial at some of these services. I started with a free trial of an online program called Constant Contact and I've been using it for the last eight years or so. It has many excellent templates that you can use to build your newsletter. You can even use Constant Contact to send a newsletter with your customized design.

Tools like Constant Contact allow you to send your newsletter to your entire list at once with a click of your mouse. The program also tracks how many people opened your newsletter and what links they clicked on. This provides you with useful information about what people are interested in, what you should do more of and what you should do less of.

A blog is another good tool for engaging with prospects. You might wonder what to write about. I suggest keeping the content very focused. When I visit a blog where the entries are so generic that they don't relate to what the writer specializes in—which is my reason for visiting in the first place—I just stop reading. Keep your topics directly related to your philosophy, your approach and your methodology. Avoid the temptation of writing about something unrelated simply for the sake of writing about something. Give your audience a reason to read.

On my website, for example, I have blog entries, each one dealing with one of the components in the Soho Sales Fundamentals methodology. Small business owners can read about these topics and find valuable tips that they can start applying to their businesses right away. My blog also gives prospects a really good sense of our approach and the philosophy behind our methodology. They can learn how we do things and see how we are different from other solution providers.

> "You need to treat these three types of customers very differently. Each type needs to be engaged to move through your sales funnel."

Social networking tools like Twitter, YouTube and Facebook are excellent ways to engage prospects. I use the Soho Sales Coaching fan page on Facebook to share my perspective on sales-related issues affecting small business owners and to encourage them to engage in dialogue. This approach could help position you as an authority or a leader in your industry, or as a spokesperson or champion for your cause. Your fans want you to have an opinion, so speak up and share it.

Don't get discouraged if you don't have a lot of fans. It's not just about the quantity of fans; it's also about the quality of conversations you have with those fans. You could have 5,000 fans on Facebook, none of whom are engaging in conversation or becoming customers. Or you could have 100 fully engaged fans, of whom a large percentage are paying customers. Which would you prefer?

All of the ideas mentioned here work well as ways to encourage prospects to give you a first try. What three things are you willing to do to motivate your prospects to become new customers?

New Customers and New Clients

To move new customers through your sales funnel, you need to engage with them in ways that motivate them to become repeat customers, or new clients. Something that I find really useful with new customers is to send them an evaluation on a monthly basis. This let's them provide feedback on how our coaching relationship is going. They can tell me what's working and what's not working, what they would like more of and what they would like less of. They can tell me how they would like my service customized for them. This type of engagement with your new customers shows that you care. It helps strengthen the relationship and increase the likelihood that new customers will want to continue with you, either with the way things are going now or with some minor changes.

Too often we sit back and assume that new customers will automatically become ongoing customers. We take them for granted. Then, as we neglect servicing them or meeting their needs, they drop us and move on to a competitor whom they think seems eager to meet their needs. If you include a question-and-answer section in your newsletter, you could publish questions from your new customers. That's a way to add value to your customers and a way to give new customers a little bit of exposure. Doing this will help transform new customers into loyal customers because they know that once they stop being a customer, their profile would no longer be in your newsletter. What are three things you could do to attract new customers to become new clients?

Maturing Clients

Maturing clients—those consumers or businesses that have purchased your products or used your services for three consecutive months—are at the top of your sales funnel. In my case, maturing clients are small business owners who I have been working with on a one-on-one basis for at least six consecutive months. Maturing clients are your best clients and the ones you need to have the highest level of engagement with. I like to spotlight these clients in my newsletter by running a photograph of them and a description of their products and services. This gives them great exposure. I also send them clippings of newspaper articles or links to web pages that I think would be of interest to them.

These small personal gestures add value to the relationship. You are trying to build the relationship in such a way that your clients could not imagine life without you. Other ways to add value to your best clients include offering them discounts on products or services, free subscriptions to industry-related magazines or publications, or introductions to prospects. What are three ways that you could encourage your maturing clients to remain loyal and refer quality leads to you?

Week 14 Action

Your task this week is to identify ways to better engage prospects, new customers, new clients and maturing clients. Establish three ways to engage them to move through your sales funnel.

Week 15 Strategy

Making Compelling Demonstrations

15

Be sure to prepare at least one week before you are scheduled to deliver a presentation. Review your prospect's website and brochures. See what search results come up for them on Yahoo! and Google. Speak with their vendors, customers and employees, if possible. Know their business first, then get your own materials ready.

Powerful Demonstrations

The sales demonstration is a time-proven strategy that strengthens your presentation by attracting the prospect's attention, stimulating interest and creating desire. Few do it better than those working in home improvement. Several years ago, I attended a home show for consumers and watched in amazement as an exhibitor demonstrated how her product used electromagnetic energy to pick up everything on the floor and in a rug from dust to dirt to detergent to dog hair. I bought two! Automobile salespeople don't simply talk about features and benefits, they hand you the keys and suggest you take the car for a spin. Pet stores are great at demonstrations too. A couple will walk into a pet store, ooh and ah over the cute kittens and buy one because a salesperson suggested, "Why don't you take one of these kittens home for the weekend? You can return the kitten on Monday morning if you don't want to keep it." Nobody ever returns a kitten!

These types of strategies give your prospect a temporary feeling of ownership that helps to build their desire for your product. In week 12, I talked about the importance of using scripts when scheduling appointments on the telephone or by email. It's equally important, if not more important, to develop a script or a presentation sequence plan for your presentations and demonstrations.

Plan Benefits in Advance

Start by asking yourself what benefits you plan on presenting or demonstrating to your prospect. Remember, there's a difference between features and benefits. Features describe what a product or service is or what it does. Benefits describe how a product or service actually helps your prospect—what's in it for them and how the product or service will add value to their life or business. Which benefits of your product or service will you demonstrate in your presentation?

In the case of my business, I help small businesses discover their ideal target customer, differentiate themselves in the marketplace and convert more leads into sales. So I focus on how this benefits my prospects. For example, I offer a Niche Discovery Worksheet that helps small businesses identify their ideal target customer. My Branding and Differentiation

Worksheet helps my customers and clients determine the top three reasons why people should choose them. I also help clients create compelling email and telephone scripts so that they can schedule more appointments. Still another is one-on-one coaching which offers structure, a format (21 weekly strategies) and accountability, which means that clients reach their goals faster.

Notice that I use bridge statements in these examples of benefits. Some bridge words I use are "so that" and "which mean". Bridge statements and bridge words help connect a feature to its benefit in the prospect's eyes.

It's also useful to check in with the prospect every now and again during your presentation by asking two questions. The first is, "Do you see how this could help businesses?" So I will often say in my presentation, "I help my clients discover their ideal target customers so that they become more focused in their marketing communication activities. Do you see how this could help businesses?" Naturally, the answer is yes. You want your prospects to get used to saying yes. This reinforces the value of your offer and makes it more likely they'll say yes when you ask for the sale. Essentially, by asking this question, you're doing a mini-close, or a trial close.

Then ask this question: "Can you see how this could help your business?" Here's an example of what I would say: "You know that I've helped clients develop compelling email and telephone scripts that have led to them scheduling more consultations with prospective clients. Do you see how this could help your business?"

Handling Objections

In preparing your presentation plan, it's useful to try to anticipate some common objections. Price is by far the most common objection across most industries. So rather than be surprised or caught off guard with this objection, spend some time thinking about your response to it. How will you handle it when a prospect objects to the price of your product or service? What might you say? You might find it useful to try to frame your response so that they'll end up saying yes and agreeing with you.

Answer the objection with a response starting with "Isn't it true that..." Sometimes even small business owners who see the importance of the work that they do with me, the value of what I offer and how I could further help them will say to me, "I'd like to try it on my own for a while." I will often respond by asking, "Isn't it true that you've already been trying it on your own for some time now and still have these challenges?" I'll continue by asking, "Since you have limited time and financial resources, wouldn't you agree that it would be a more effective use of your time and money working together doing it better and faster, so you can focus on what you do best, which is running your business?" Brainstorm the most common objections that you've experienced and anticipate hearing during your presentation and spend some time writing your answers to them. Frame your answers positively with a response starting with "Isn't it true that...?" or "Wouldn't you agree that...?"

Plan Materials in Advance

You need to write out what type of demonstration and presentation materials you're planning on using. Are you going to use a brochure, a flip chart, a binder, your laptop? Or are you going to direct prospects to a website? These are all great materials and none of them is better or worse than the other. Just be sure that you are crystal clear about what materials you're going to use and that those materials are of the best quality. If you're going to be using a brochure or a binder, make sure it's crisp and clean and brand new. Not some tattered old thing that you've been marking up with dog-ears for the past two years. Remember, you are a professional.

Here are some examples of demonstration and presentation materials that I've used. Most of my consultations are conducted over the telephone and the Internet is a big part of my work because most of my clients are scattered around the globe. I want my presentation to simulate our working relationship as closely as possible. It is important that I use the telephone and the Internet during my presentation and demonstration, because that helps show my prospects how easily sales coaching works.

I typically send prospects a sheet and video that describes Soho Sales Coaching. These items contain information on who we help, what we do, my background, testimonials and media exposure. I go through that one sheet with my prospect, highlighting certain things I think they will find useful based on their specific challenges. To further demonstrate how I can help, I often send them a link to some videos on YouTube that feature short clips on topics that I've addressed during speaking engagements. I typically direct prospects to a video that addresses their specific challenge. This positions me as an expert and an authority and adds an experiential component to the presentation.

I also send prospects the Soho Sales Fundamentals self-assessment, which is a diagnostic tool I've created that outlines twenty-one benchmarks against which to measure their sales strategy against. During my presentation, I walk prospects through a few of the benchmarks that I believe are most relevant to their business. Again, this helps position me as the authority on small business sales. I've also created a Prospecting Activity Calculator that is used to determine a prospect's income and goals along with ways to measure their activity. I demonstrate this tool during my presentation as well.

Keep your list of demonstration materials in front of you during your presentation. Make sure to have those materials ready to go either at your fingertips or at the click of a mouse.

Use Proof Devices

It's also useful to list the stories of similar situations that you plan to mention during a presentation. Every prospect seems to think that their business or their challenges are so unique that you've never seen anything like it before. What you need to do is to demonstrate that you've actually helped people in similar situations. You do that by telling short stories. Write down the names of clients you've helped in similar industries or in similar situations. What were the challenges they faced? What strategies did you use to help them overcome those challenges and what were the results? That is the story you tell.

Such stories are known as "proof devices" that make it easier for your prospective clients to say yes. After telling your story is a great time to ask, "Do you see how this could help your business?"

Strategies that create physical involvement in your presentation or demonstration on the part of your prospect are also proof devices. Such strategies engage your prospects and make presentations and demonstrations even more powerful. So rather than just talk about the car you're selling, actually give the keys to the prospect so that they can go for a test ride. If you're selling photocopiers, have your prospects demonstrate how they work. Give them a piece of paper and ask them to make copies or scans so they can get a real feel for how the machine works and see for themselves how easy it is to use.

The same principle about getting prospects physically involved holds true when selling services too. How can you get someone physically involved in a service? Well, if you're in the financial services industry, one idea is to give them a piece of paper and a pen and ask them to write a few things down or to calculate some things.

In my case with prospects, once their annual income goal is clear, I ask them to write out some calculations from the Prospecting Activity Calculator. For example, if they want to earn $120,000 per year, I ask them to write down how much that is per month: $10,000.

Then I ask them to write down how much they charge per client each month. If they earn $1,000 per client per month, they'll need ten clients per month to achieve their income goals. How many prospecting calls do they need to make in order to get ten clients? Let's assume a 50 percent closing ratio. Typically, to get ten clients, they're going to have to deliver twenty presentations or submit twenty proposals. I have them write that down.

> "Risk causes prospects to hesitate. Proof devices help your prospects reduce their perceived risk of buying."

Let's assume that 10 percent of the people within their circle of influence meet their qualifying criteria. In order to make twenty presentations, they will likely have to contact two hundred prospects. Remember, these two hundred prospects are not random people. They must have a need for the product, the ability to afford it and the authority to make a buying decision. Then I ask prospects to divide those two hundred prospects per month by twenty business days per month. Now they see that they will need to contact ten qualified prospects per day.

Helping prospects see their business through the lens of the Prospecting Activity Calculator positions me as an expert. As we go through the exercise, prospects experience something they may never have experienced before and they become physically involved in the presentation. This increases the likelihood that they will want to work with me. It helps to engage them.

Remember, when you're using a proof device as a way to structure your presentation, as in the example of the Prospecting

Activity Calculator, make sure that the conversation flows naturally and that you are guiding the process.

Confidence in Your Product

Proof devices help reinforce or restore confidence in your product, your business and yourself because they help your prospect reduce their perceived risk of buying. Risk causes prospects to hesitate or reconsider buying. Your challenge is to anticipate, discover and eliminate risks—real or perceived.

Risks show up in prospects' minds through thoughts like these: "Maybe it's not worth it. I'm afraid I can't afford it. Maybe I don't really need it. I'm afraid of being overcharged. What if it doesn't work? What if it falls apart? I'm afraid they won't support me. Maybe there's something better." Basically, prospects are afraid of the consequences of making the wrong decision.

Through proof devices, prospects feel more comfortable about deciding to buy. Proof devices that reduce prospects' perceived risk of buying need to be part of your presentation. You could try offering your prospects free samples. You could offer them a tour of your factory or your office or show them photos. Explain your product by showing prospects photos, brochures, portfolios, catalogs, charts, or test results. Show them a small model of your product if it's too large to actually demonstrate in person. You could offer a money back guarantee. Let prospects know that they can always bring your product back if it doesn't work. Let them know that you help people like them all the time. Let them know that you'll match any quoted price for up to thirty days.

Be sure to provide testimonials from happy customers. One way of getting testimonials is by asking your past and present customers, "Of all the people that you could have worked with, what are the main reasons that you chose me over other solution providers?" Whenever one of your customers sends you an email thanking you for something, edit what they wrote (if necessary), show the edited version to them and ask them if you can use it as a testimonial.

Asking your prospects to list and compare the risks and rewards they anticipate from purchasing your product or service could also help them make the decision to buy. Making a compelling demonstration of how your product or service can help prospects overcome their challenges and using proof devices will make it easier for prospects to say yes.

Week 15 Action

Your task this week is to make compelling demonstrations. Plan your benefits, your answers to objections and your materials in advance. This will help prospects to gain confidence in your product, your business and yourself.

Week 16 Strategy

Choosing Your Top Three Closing Techniques

16

Closing the sale is not difficult if everything is handled properly throughout your presentation. Effective closing methods do not pressure the prospect. Rather, effective closing methods focus on prospects' dominant buying motives.

When large, complex sales are involved, try to achieve incremental commitments. By this I mean, ask your prospect to make small commitments at first so that over time they become willing to make larger commitments. If they're not in a position to say yes to purchasing a major, complex product that's very expensive, perhaps they could make a commitment to get back to you by a certain date, or to read your proposal by a certain date, or to meet with you again on a certain date. Avoid pressuring the prospect; yet at the same time, get them to make commitments they can say yes to.

Avoid Surprises

So often people go through a presentation talking about the features and benefits of their product or service but neglecting to mention the price. Then, right at the end of the presentation, at the close of the sale, the prospect is shocked at how expensive the product is. Why are they shocked? Because that is the first time they've heard the price. Your prospect should have been given a clear idea of what their investment will be right from the beginning. This is all part of qualifying your prospect from the start.

When someone approaches me for sales training or sales coaching, I let them know up front what a typical investment in training or coaching would be. I ask them directly, "Can you afford this at this time?" If the answer is no, then I know they are not a prospect. When people answer no to that question, you need to stop talking to them. If the answer is yes, you continue talking with them by showing them what they get for that investment. Prospects need at least a ballpark figure from the start. You want to avoid surprises at the close. It's a lot easier to demonstrate value than it is to make concessions on price.

Ask Four Times

Don't give up after asking for the sale once. I've heard that 80 percent of salespeople give up after asking for the sale only once. I've also heard that 80 percent of sales occur when people ask for the sale four times. So if you want to know the fastest and easiest way to increase your sales, the answer is simple: Ask four times!

Children are masters of closing techniques. When a child wants something in the grocery store, they'll ask for it (close). Parents may say no (objection). But the child doesn't give up. They'll usually ask, "Why not?" (asking to clarify the objection). Parents may explain that it's unhealthy (clarifying the objection). The child responds by saying it must be ok if other kids are eating it (proof device). They'll ask for the food again (close). The parent responds by saying no (objection). The child asks why not again (asking to clarify the objection). The parent responds with, "Because I said so!" (clarifying the objection). The child starts crying or screaming. Here parents sometimes give in because they perceive the reward of having the child stop crying is greater than the risk of buying the sugary cereal. The child has closed the sale!

I'm not suggesting that you have a tantrum when your prospect does not want to buy. But you get the point. The quickest way for you to increase your sales is to simply ask for the sale several times during your presentation. Understand and answer your prospects' objections, taking into account what they perceive as risks and rewards.

Pay Attention to Buying Signals

If you are showing a house and your clients start talking about how they can visualize their things in the house, you know they can see the value. This is a signal that they may be ready to buy. And that is your signal to start asking prompting questions that will lead to closing the sale.

I've talked to many salespeople in many stores who haven't noticed my buying signals. I'll be in an electronics store, let's say, looking at a big screen television. I'll make a positive buying statement like, "Well, this would look great on my TV stand." I'll ask the salesperson questions about cash payment discounts or how quickly the TV can be delivered. The salesperson will answer my questions, of course. But then he'll say, "Well, if you have anymore questions, you can find me over in the video camera section." That salesperson just blew it! He lost the opportunity to close a sale. The next thing I do is walk out of that store and head to another store. There a salesperson who acts on my verbal and nonverbal cues will close the sale for the big screen TV. Paying attention to verbal signals and body language that tell you when your prospects are ready to buy is vital to closing the sale.

Closing the Sale

So what are some specific methods of closing the sale? One way is to ask prospects what they would like to do now. For instance, often when I am speaking to a prospect after my presentation and they seem interested, I will ask them, "So what would you like to do now?" I might also ask, "When would you like to get started?" That question is more presumptive than the first example. Or I might say, "All you need to get started right now is a deposit." You could try addressing the issue of deposits by saying, "Clients typically make full payment in advance or make a 50 percent initial deposit. Which would you prefer?" Most clients will opt for the 50 percent deposit, which is what you wanted anyway, isn't it? Notice that you're framing the conversation around the amount of the initial deposit, not around the issue of making an initial deposit. If you've earned a prospect's respect and built a strong relationship with them, you could even begin writing up the order and ask which address you should send the invoice to.

Common Objections

Objections usually have to do with the amount of money, time, or effort involved in a product or service or with its degree of effectiveness. Some common objections include:

- It's too expensive.
- It takes too long.
- I'm too busy.
- It costs too much.
- It won't work for me.
- I can't wait for it.
- It's going to be difficult.

How do you handle objections? It might help you to understand that in sales when a prospect says no what they really mean is not yet. I'm not ready to buy yet. I'm not convinced yet. You haven't demonstrated the value yet. I don't understand exactly how this works yet. That's what they're saying. Your job is to make things clear to the prospect and to remember they are not saying no to you, they are saying no to this opportunity at this time.

Perhaps you've heard the expression that a confused mind always says no. To help your prospects say yes, you have to clarify the information. Make sure you are crystal clear about their challenges and that they are crystal clear about your solution to their problems. Ask them every step of the way,

"Can you see how this helps businesses? Can you see how this could help your business?"

Clarifying Price Objections

In my experience, price objections can mean one of two things. When a prospect says your product or service is too expensive, they could mean they can't afford it or don't have the budget for it. Another meaning is that they can afford it and they do have the budget, but they don't think the product or service is worth the price. They don't see the value in your offering.

Here's an example of the first meaning. Say you walked into a Maserati dealership and were just noticing the price when a salesperson came up to you and asked, "Would you like to purchase this car?" The answer for a lot of people would be, "No, it's too expensive." You may see the value, you may think it's worth it, but you just can't afford it.

Here's an example of the second meaning. Suppose someone offered to sell you a beat up old lemon of a car that's all rusted and has a bumper falling off. When you're told that the price is $5,000 and asked if you want to buy the car, you might say, "No, it's too expensive." The seller might respond by asking, "Oh, you can't afford that price? Is it over your budget?" And you might answer, "Well, of course I can afford that price. I just don't think it's worth it for that piece of junk."

These are two very distinct objections that need to be handled differently. Your job is to clarify which of the two interpretations of a price objection you are dealing with. You can do this by saying to your prospect, "When you say it's too expensive, do you mean that it's out of your price range or more than you're expecting to spend today? Or do you mean that you haven't seen the value and you don't think it's worth it?" Then just listen for their answer. Once you understand the objection, address it appropriately. If the objection is an issue of affordability, talk with the prospect about payment plans, a deposit, deferred payment, or a layaway plan. If the objection is about the worth or value of your product or service, talk with the prospect about what would make it more valuable to them. Ask, "What can we do to add value to this so that it would be worth the investment?"

> "If you haven't sold your prospects on the "yes", then they have sold you on the "no". Regardless of who has been paid, a sale has been made."

You also need to ask if this objection is a deal breaker. This is important for you to know so that you don't spend a lot of time trying to address the objection if it's really not that big a deal. Imagine, for example, that you're a realtor showing a house to a couple and one of them says, "I wish there was a bit more closet space." The location of the house is great, the price is good, the house is in an up-and-coming neighborhood and the property is undervalued. You need to find out how important closet space is to the couple. Simply ask, "Is the issue of closet space a deal breaker?" If the answer is no, move on to something else.

Respond to both types of price objections by using proof devices or similar situation examples. Then ask for the sale again. At the same time, be willing to recognize a hopeless selling situation and avoid saying anything that will jeopardize the relationship in the future.

Practice Makes Perfect

It would be useful for you to list the common objections people have given you in the past and then to write a short rationale for each objection. Frame your response to each objection in a positive way and practice it. Think of examples of clients that had the same objection, found a way to overcome it and consequently benefited from using your products and services. Include these similar situation stories in your response.

For example, you could say, "I can understand why you might feel that the product is expensive. In fact, one of my clients felt the very same way initially but thought it would be a good idea to take advantage of our 100 percent money back guarantee so that they could try the product risk free. Once they started with us, they noticed how easily the product worked and they started getting a great return on their investment." If you haven't sold your prospects on the "yes", then they have sold you on the "no". Regardless of who has been paid, a sale has been made.

Practice saying out loud your responses to objections so that you'll feel confident when prospects raise concerns. Also, make sure that your marketing material includes your pricing. That makes it a lot easier for you to address concerns. Role playing with a coach, an associate, or a teammate is the best way to experience the feelings that accompany responding to objections and closing the sale. You could also practice by yourself with a video recorder.

Knowing your top three closing techniques and getting comfortable with them is a key factor in becoming better at sales. The list of common objections and your responses to those objections is equally important. Both of these strategies could accelerate the selling process so that you can move your relationship with a prospect to the next stage.

After the Sale

Sometimes new customers experience buyer's remorse. To help prevent this, be sure to reassure the customer that they've made the right decision and remind them why they made that decision in the first place.

Remember to ask customers for referrals by asking them who else they know could benefit from what they are now enjoying. Hand them a piece of paper and a pen so they can jot down two or three names and the contact information while they're still in a good mood. Follow up with a thank you letter (for mature clients) or a welcome letter (for new clients).

Week 16 Action

Your task this week is to create your top three closing techniques. Avoid surprises, pay attention to buying signals and ask for the sale four times. This could accelerate the selling process.

Relationship Fundamentals

17

Week 17 Strategy

Focusing on the Future

Over the past ten years, people have been giving me feedback (both negative and positive) on my one-on-one sales coaching sessions and my in-house corporate sales training. Receiving feedback presents me with great opportunities to learn what my customers really need and then to make changes to improve my business. Listening to my clients and acting to implement improvements helps to keep my business viable for the future.

Learning from Your Clients

Caring about what's important to your clients is a way to develop strong relationships with them. You can demonstrate that you care by asking your customers questions. Of course, it can be scary asking for feedback, because you're not asking your customers what they love about you, you're asking them about their impression of you. If you're courageous enough to ask, the reward is priceless.

An excellent way to learn from your customers is to use a Client Evaluation Form. Use this form to ask your clients specific questions around your work together. I like asking people scale questions. So, for example, to assess the value of your work together, ask them to rate the following on a scale one to five (1 = not at all; 5 = absolutely):

- I am achieving the goals I intended to.
- I am achieving additional worthwhile goals.
- I now produce results faster and easier.
- I now have skills that I will benefit from.

How clients rate themselves on these questions clearly shows the value they are receiving from your work together.

You could also ask your clients specific questions about you as a service provider, which they answer with the same scale of one to five:

- The provider is a model for me on the perspective to achieve.
- I trust my provider completely.
- The provider always treats me with respect.
- The provider is rigorous and committed to my success.
- The provider is on time and present.
- The provider is available when needed.
- Within a month of starting, I felt confident in the provider.

These questions help answer how effective you are personally as their service provider.

You could also ask general questions. For example, "Do you have any other ideas, insights, or suggestions on ways that my service could improve?" I think it is important to ask if any of their initial expectations have not been met. The answer to that question will give you a clear indication of where you might have fallen short or where you should have clarified expectations earlier on.

That question leads nicely into the next question on your Client Evaluation Form: "What do you want most from our future partnership and what would keep this process rewarding?" Here you're basically asking clients what they need to continue working with you.

It's also useful to ask clients how they feel about continuing to work with your organization. You could give clients these choices:

- Excellent, let's continue as we are.
- Good, but I'd like to discuss some changes in how we work.
- I want to continue but with a different approach.
- This isn't working for me. I want to stop.

These choices put it all on the line and clarify for you how things stand in your client's view.

Some of the feedback you get from customers will be hard to hear. No one likes to hear that they haven't met their customers' expectations. But avoiding asking for feedback because you might be told something unpleasant will not help you grow a successful business and reach your long-term goals. The alternative to not asking for feedback is having your unsatisfied customers quietly leave you for a competitor who is willing

> “We cannot control what goes on outside our businesses, but we can (and must!) control what goes on inside them.”

to ask them about their specific needs. And that's not really an alternative at all.

The way to keep customers happy is to learn from past mistakes and then to focus. on how you can make improvements in the future. Don't spend time beating yourself up over shortcomings. Instead, the next time a prospect turns down your proposal or a current client leaves you for a competitor, try looking at the situation objectively and seeing the opportunity for growth. What lessons could you learn? How could you make improvements to your business that could benefit customers in the future?

Taking Personal Responsibility

Another aspect of focusing on the future and how to improve is taking personal responsibility for results. Blaming an economic downturn for a decrease in business leads to the logic of crediting an economic upturn for an increase in business. I'm an eternal optimist in that I believe the future is something we can control despite challenging economic times. We cannot control what goes on outside our businesses, but we can (and must!) control what goes on inside them.

One of the tools that you could use is a Weekly Activity Worksheet. The worksheet lists your revenue and volume goals (number of customers) and breaks those goals down into the following daily activities:

- Hours spent calling (#).
- Prospecting calls (#).
- Presentations scheduled (#).
- Presentations delivered (#).
- Revenue target achieved ($).
- Volume target achieved (#).
- Hours spent calling (#) / revenue earned ($).
- Prospecting calls made last month (#) / revenue earned this month ($).

The worksheet demonstrates a direct relationship between today's efforts and tomorrow's rewards. It will be hard to succeed in the future if you're procrastinating in the present. Measuring your weekly activities will help you take responsibility for results, both good and bad.

One way to overcome procrastination is to make a list of your priorities. As a small business owner, you should only be focusing on two things: what is important today and what is important in the future. Everything else should be delegated or eliminated. When you're feeling overwhelmed by your list of things to do, look at each task and determine which category it belongs in. Then ask yourself this question: What three things do I need to accomplish today, in order for today to be a success? By making a priority of focusing on the three most important things for today, you will become more efficient (doing things right) and effective (doing the right things) than you ever thought possible.

Week 17 Action

Your task this week is to focus on the future. Create a client evaluation form.

Week 18 Strategy

18 Having a Positive Attitude

It's so important to have a positive attitude because a negative attitude becomes a self-fulfilling prophecy. This reminds me of the expression that goes something like, "Whether you believe you will fail or succeed, you're right." This expression may sound innocuous, but it actually points to some serious consequences for business owners. If you're wondering why you're struggling to make sales, the first thing you should check is your attitude. Perhaps you'll notice that you have a negative attitude about yourself, your products or services, or your customers, current economic conditions and the state of the world. Unattended to, your negative attitude will become your reality and you will fail. To succeed, you must correct it.

Imagine that two equally knowledgeable, skilled and capable people are offering the same product or service. One has a positive attitude while the other has a negative attitude. I can almost guarantee that the one with a more positive attitude will outperform the one with a negative attitude every time. So check your attitude.

Success Breeds Success

What can you do to improve your attitude? Sometimes awareness alone is not enough. Try drawing upon past successes and remembering what worked.

When I was a financial services representative years ago, I went to meetings with prospects believing that they would sign up right then and there. And usually they did. This belief wasn't arrogance on my part but rather confidence based on past experience. I loved our product and I knew that it helped clients achieve their goals. I was knowledgeable about our product (and those of our competitors) and confident in my ability to articulate the features and benefits. Because I was able to draw upon past successes helping parents invest in their children's post-secondary education, I had no reason to doubt that I could repeat those results on each sales call I made. Success breeds success.

You're Just Adding Zeros

You might be wondering what to do if you've never had success in this area. Maybe you've never sold a certain type of product or service before. Maybe you're new to sales altogether. Here you need to tap into some other past successes. Surely you've had some accomplishments or achievements in other areas. Draw upon those for motivation and inspiration. What did you do well in order to achieve that goal? What inner quality did you call on to succeed? Was it courage? Resourcefulness? Speedy responsiveness? Was it attentiveness, curiosity, knowledge? There is little difference between a $100 sale and a $1,000 sale. And little difference between a $1,000 sale and a $10,000 sale. And so on. If you can sell something for $100, you can sell something for $10,000 (or more) as long as you can demonstrate the value. The selling process is the same. You're just adding zeros.

No Excuses

Getting better at your craft will help you improve your confidence and develop a more positive attitude. Go back to basics. Learn more about your product and service. After you've read this book and done the exercises, read it again. Working with a coach could help you incorporate these tools into your everyday behavior so they become habits.

One way of having a positive attitude is to make sure that you're interacting with positive people in a good environment. Misery loves company and miserable people love to bring you down to their level. Stay away from complainers and whiners. They are only making excuses for their failure and hoping that you'll give them permission to fail. By playing their game, you're actually giving yourself

"If you can sell something for $100, you can sell something for $10,000 (or more) as long as you can demonstrate the value. You're just adding zeros."

permission to fail. Don't get sucked in. Instead, spend your time learning from winners.

How conducive is your working environment to success? Look around your office and make sure you have the tools of the trade that you need. Do you have a comfortable chair? Do you have a fast and reliable Internet connection? What about a computer with all of the software applications you need? If you find yourself starting sentences with, "If I only had", then it's time for you to get off your butt and go and get it. No excuses.

Week 18 Action

Your task this week is to have a positive attitude. Write down your greatest sales achievement. You'll be able to draw upon that for motivation and inspiration.

Week 19 Strategy

Developing Your "Expert Power"

19

What exactly is your "expert power"? This is specific knowledge that differentiates you from your competitors offering similar products and services. In this day and age, there are so many people out there doing the same thing that the marketplace is confusing for buyers. Your customers don't know who's better or why. They can't tell the players in the marketplace apart. In order for you to differentiate yourself, you need to stand out from the competition. One way of standing out is to become an expert in your field instead of simply a salesperson.

Keep Learning

I want to take a moment to applaud you for investing your time in reading this book. By doing so, you're taking a step toward developing yourself professionally. This is a step that says, "I'm investing time in reading this book because I need to get better at increasing sales in my small business." You may even be considering developing your skills further by receiving coaching or sales training. Making a commitment to improving yourself will enhance your expert power.

You should also be taking courses to increase your competency in other areas such as self-confidence, public speaking, managing your business and knowledge of your industry. You always need to be learning. Whenever you find yourself in a slump, see that as an opportunity for you to get back to basics. Consider what you could learn next or what you're ready to review.

If you're like me, you probably have a bookcase full of sales, marketing, management, leadership and communication books. Have you read them all? Have you read any of them lately? I like to re-read books after several months or years. It's almost like the book I'm re-reading is brand new, because I'm in a different place from where I was when I first read the book. You might not have been ready to fully absorb some of the lessons delivered in a book you read a few years ago. Picking up that same book today, you'll probably learn new lessons that you'll be ready to start applying right away. So take a fresh look at your bookshelf or visit the bookstore or the library. I guarantee you'll find a book with just the right information which is suited to where you are now in your learning.

Having a Coach

One of the best ways for you to develop your expert power is to learn from other experts. Do you have a coach? No? Get one! I've been running my own business for more than ten years, but I've only really begun to taste success in the past three years. The early years of running my business were a real struggle. I was working hard, spending a lot of money on advertising, trying to get business where I could, with only average results. How was it that I could have been working so hard and putting out so much effort and still not seen results?

It comes down to the difference between attitude and aptitude. It's sort of like having the positive energy, drive and determination to see a sunset, but your strategy is to walk east. You have the heart, but you don't have the brain. I was so frustrated and was about to give up when I received an email from a coach who specializes in coaching coaches. (How's that for finding a niche market?) I had been receiving emails from this person for a couple of years but had stubbornly felt that I could do things on my own. Now, two years later, I was no better off than I was before. I thought to myself, "I don't want to quit my business until I've tried absolutely everything."

> "One of the best ways for you to develop your expert power is to learn from other experts. Do you have a coach? No? Get one!"

I decided that trying everything would include signing up for this trainer's one-year coaching program. It seemed to be a good value for the money and I could afford it. I remember thinking that at that point, I really didn't have much else to loose but everything to gain if this coach's program worked. I remember telling my girlfriend (who's now my wife) that it would be my "make it or break it" year. I was going to throw everything and the kitchen sink at this and commit to the process 100 percent.

I learned so much about myself and about my business by going through that coaching process. My coach helped me zero in on my ideal target customer and decide on some effective ways of reaching them. Through him I learned some important lessons about always challenging myself to play a bigger game. Applying what I learned through working with that coach has meant that I've had to constantly set new goals, because I've been blowing the older ones out of the water!

My level of self-confidence is high because I make a priority of always learning more about sales and small business. All I do is study and share what I've learned with my clients. This helps me feel more comfortable in myself as an expert in small business sales.

Enhancing Your Expert Power

What else could you do to enhance your expert power? Consider joining an industry association and begin working toward a professional designation. I'm a member of the Association of Professional Speakers Singapore, Business Network International, International Coach Federation and Marketing Institute of Singapore. I regularly attend their monthly membership meetings as well as their monthly peer coaching meetings. The peer coaching meetings are conducted in a format that helps us as professionals to fine tune and polish our coaching skills.

What course could you register for today? Who could you engage as a mentor or coach? Remember that actively pursuing personal and / or professional development activities will develop your expert power and improve your sales performance.

Week 19 Action

Your task this week is to develop your expert power. Consider registering for a course, joining an organization, or hiring a coach. This will help you become an expert in your field and increase sales.

Week 20 Strategy

Improving Your Communication Style

20

Studies suggest the small role played by words in the communication process. Words alone account for only 7 percent of people's impression of you. What people hear makes up 38 percent of their impression. And what people see or feel accounts for 55 percent of the impression they form. In order for you to be effective in sales, you need to have a communication style that speaks effectively to prospects. Your voice quality and volume, how articulate you are, the way you dress, your posture, how you walk, your handshake—these all form powerful and lasting impressions with prospects. How is your communication style helping or hurting you?

Image Is Everything

I remember something that happened several years ago during a trip to Trinidad with my family. We checked into a hotel and the first thing I did was see if they had tennis courts and a tennis pro. Those of you who know me know that I'm crazy about tennis. Seeking out courts and a pro is always the first thing I do when I arrive at a new hotel. To my delight, this hotel had both. So I set up an appointment with the hitting pro and got ready for my lesson. I was so excited that I ran down to the courts with my racket and tennis bag and eagerly awaited the appearance of my hitting pro.

As I was looking into the distance, I saw a man strolling lazily toward me. Here was my tennis instructor, a good fifty pounds overweight and with a beer belly bursting out of his tennis shirt! The brochure in the hotel room had implied that the tennis pro was a young, slender athlete who was a former member of the Davis cup team. Now Trinidad has never been known as a tennis powerhouse, but making it onto your Davis cup team for your national tennis team is quite an accomplishment by any standard. So I was expecting a pro in tiptop shape. I was disappointed.

I was about to turn around and run from the courts when I heard him yell out my name: "Tom!" I replied, "Yes, Coach" and reluctantly walked with him to the tennis court. To my astonishment, he kicked my butt! My parents still sometimes remind me of how badly that hitting pro beat me. So did I form a wrong first impression of him? Of course I did and I was wrong to judge. But to be honest, if I hadn't prepaid for the lesson, I may in fact have run for the hills the moment I saw him sauntering toward me.

First Impressions

How is your first impression with prospects helping or hurting you? When you enter a room, you need to believe and project that you have a reason to be there and something important to say. Your confidence will suggest that the meeting will benefit your prospect. Notice how you execute your entrance and the manner in which you carry yourself. Is this communicating the importance of what you have to say?

A healthy handshake establishes the business relationship, signals active participation and gives the message of confidence and goodwill. Imagine, then, what a weak grip or a bone-crushing grip could be communicating to your prospect. Eye contact is one of the best ways of saying, "I'm listening." But prolonged eye contact can be threatening. Nodding occasionally when your prospect speaks also indicates that you are listening and conveys agreement.

75 Percent of People Don't Like You

The reason why 75 percent of people don't like you is because people tend to adopt their own preferred communication style. And people tend to like people who remind them of themselves. We typically fall into one of four communication styles based on two factors. Those two factors are your level of sociability and your level of dominance. "SOHO" is a quadrant model and an acronym for the four communication styles: Supportive, Open, Hurried and Organized.

The Supportive communication style tends to have a low level of dominance and a high level of sociability. Supporters tend to be good listeners, to not be forceful and to avoid conflict. They usually share their feelings in a non-overly assertive way; they prefer friendly persuasion to direct disagreement or conflict.

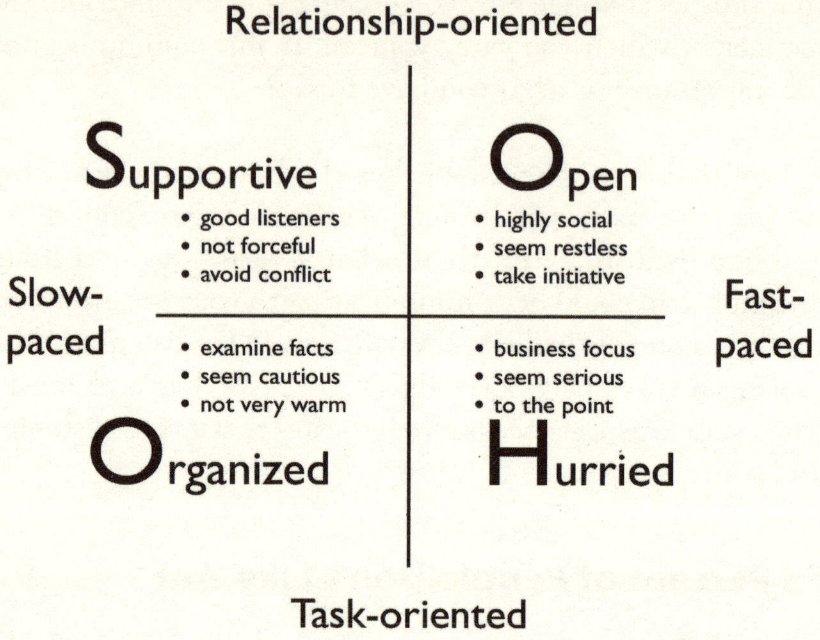

The Open communication style has both a high level of sociability and a high level of dominance. Openers tend to be expressive and excitable; they can sometimes seem restless. They tend to take the initiative in situations. Openers build social relationships and friendships quickly. They are willing to share personal stories and are often quite informal in their interactions with people.

The Hurried communication style has a high level of dominance and a low level of sociability. Hurriers tend to be demanding, aggressive, determined and frank. They tend to want to get straight to the point, do more talking than listening and seem quite serious. They like to get down to business and they can come across as being more transaction oriented than friendly.

The Organized communication style has a low level of sociability and a low level of dominance. Organizers tend to be reserved and cautious. They like to examine the facts carefully. They like order. Organizers often seem controlled in their emotions and not very warm in their communication.

Do you recognize yourself in any of these four communication styles? Which one best fits your approach? Which one of these communication styles do you think you like the most or the least in other people? Take some time to think about this.

Style Flexing

I remember once when I was delivering a sales training workshop for an organization, one of their sales representatives asked which one of these communication styles is most effective for a salesperson. My answer was, all of them! The reason is simple. People like people who are like them. People relate more easily to people who are like them. People do business with people they know, like and trust. So it would seem the easiest way to get people to like you is to be like them! This is known as style flexing.

Your job as a sales professional is to help your prospect feel as comfortable as possible. This means communicating with them in a manner in which they feel comfortable. Here are some tips about the most effective ways of communicating with Supporters, Openers, Hurriers and Organizers.

Supporters are thoughtful and deliberate and are unlikely to tell you directly that they're not interested. Don't push them to make a decision quickly. Instead, ask them to make smaller

> "People do business with people they know, like and trust. So it would seem the easiest way to get people to like you is to be like them!"

incremental commitments so that you can gauge their genuine level of interest. Openers love focusing on the big picture and making quick decisions. Avoid overwhelming them with details and paperwork. Get excited when speaking with Openers! And loosen up!

Hurriers like getting down to business, so avoid social chitchat and get to the point quickly. Be sure to ask a lot of questions, because Hurriers love to talk. Avoid the temptation to sell your business so that you don't end up talking too much yourself. Don't overwhelm Hurriers with details; they make decisions quickly based on summaries of key facts.

Organizers are generally quite cautious; be sure to give them lots of backup information to help them make decisions. They like to take their time making decisions, though. Let them take the time they need to analyze everything thoroughly. Don't push them. A confused mind always says no, so with Organizers, err on the side of too much information rather than too little.

Over the next few days or weeks, practice recognizing the four communication styles by paying close attention to your social interactions. Ask yourself, "Is the person I'm speaking with a Supporter, Opener, Hurrier, or Organizer?" Noticing how dominant and sociable they are will help you pinpoint their communication style. If someone has a high level of dominance, they could be an Opener or a Hurrier. Note their sociability; if they tend to be more on the passive side, they are either Supporters or Organizers.

Remember, improving your communication style, manners, voice quality, nonverbal communication and style flexing all contribute to your success in personal selling.

Week 20 Action

Your task this week is to improve your communication style. Pinpoint the communication styles of your prospects by noticing how dominant and sociable they are. Style flexing will make it easier for people to relate to you.

Week 21 Strategy

Establishing Strong Relationships

21

A salesperson can compete on the basis of product, price and service but still lose the sale because of the relationship between the customer and a competitor's salesperson. As I mentioned in the previous chapter, people buy from people they know, like and trust. Your likeability and your ability to form strong relationships quickly will be more effective than all the credentials in the world or even having the lowest price.

Partnering Relationships

With the increased competition and greater product and service complexity of today's marketplace, there is a need to adopt a relationship strategy that emphasizes the lifetime customer. Instead of viewing prospects as transactional customers that you sell to once, you view them as partners in a long-term selling relationship.

When I'm speaking with an organization about delivering sales training and coaching, I discuss not only the date of the upcoming training for their sales team, but also how I can partner with them to help all the sales teams and their various offices around the world, throughout the year and in years to come. Partnering can be defined as a strategically developed, long-term relationship that focuses on solving the customers' buying problems. Partnering is the highest quality selling relationship.

There are three keys to a partnering relationship: the relationship is built on shared values; everyone clearly understands the purpose of the partnership and is committed to the vision; and the role of the salesperson moves from selling to supporting. By demonstrating over time how you can support your customers in solving their problems, you will never sell another day in your life.

Four Key Groups

Your relationship strategy needs to focus on four key groups: customers, secondary decision makers, your company support staff and your management personnel. You need the support of these people to help you reach your goals. What are you doing to establish, build and maintain relationships with people in those key groups? One way to develop stronger connections with those people is to help them. Think about the ways you are already helping them. Then find out what else they need to reach their goals and help them with that. People will respond to you helping them with similar benevolence of their own.

Getting Testimonials

When we talk about how great we are it can come across as bragging, but when other people talk about us it comes across as evidence. This is why testimonials are so effective. Testimonials are one way that customers reciprocate for the support you give them.

Your big challenge is to develop a strategy that will help you get more testimonials. Most people don't ask for testimonials and when they do they wait until after a project has been completed. Take a look at your list of past customers. Have you asked them all for testimonials? Why not? And what about the clients you are working with right now? I'm guessing they've said kind words about you during your time together, right?

Try practicing this. The next time one of your customers sends you an email or tells you on the telephone about how happy they are with what you're currently doing for them or how you have recently helped them, thank them very much and mention that what they just said is something that could be really useful for other people to know about your business. Ask them if you could use exactly what they just told you as a testimonial. More often than not, the customer will say yes—and there you go, you got yourself a testimonial. Easy! You could even take the liberty of writing something up in your own words, sending it to a past or current client and asking them if they would feel comfortable signing off on it or putting it on their letterhead. Tell them that you appreciate how busy they are and you thought that you would draft a few things based on what they had told you before.

I remember being approached by one company that asked me to submit a proposal by the end of the day. I wanted to put my best foot forward, so I fired off emails requesting testimonials to two of my most recent clients for whom I had delivered sales training.

For one company, I drafted a testimonial based on something they had said in previous correspondence and asked them if they would agree with it. The managing director said that he wanted to rework it in his own words and would get back to me by the end of the day. His version was ten times better than the one that I had sent him.

> "When we talk about how great we are it can come across as bragging, but when other people talk about us it comes across as evidence."

In the case of the second company, the chairman had announced to all the salespeople immediately after my training that in his thirty years in sales and having received and delivered many trainings, mine was probably the best he had ever participated in. Naturally, that was the testimonial that I asked to receive in writing. With these two testimonials included in my proposal, do you think I got the job? Obviously!

Getting Referrals

Referrals are another way that customers reciprocate. The great thing about referrals is that they don't cost anything and they come with a high level of trust built in. Like a testimonial, a referral carries a high degree of credibility.

While most business people and salespeople say they would prefer to receive customers through word of mouth, many of them haven't created a strategy around getting referrals. So they end up waiting by the phone or checking their email in hopes of getting referral business. Hope is not a strategy.

So what can you do right away to get more referrals? Ask your current clients. Ask your former clients. Ask prospects who turned you down. You might be wondering why I'm telling you to ask prospects who turned down the opportunity to work with you. Well, they may have declined to hire you for any number of reasons—perhaps they couldn't afford you, they didn't have the budget at the time, the timing wasn't right for them to proceed, or their priorities changed. But they could still see value in what you offer. And in fact they may know two or three companies that actually are in a position to move forward with you and could benefit from your services.

Part of developing your strategy is sensing the right timing. No one likes to be surprised or put in an uncomfortable position by being asked aggressively for referrals. It's useful if you can set the stage during your initial conversations or meetings with prospects to let them know what to expect. Try saying something like, "Now that you are looking into our services, you'll probably start noticing a lot of other businesses that could benefit from this sort of service. In the same way that you came to my business through a referral from a good friend of yours, I would like to ask you from time to time if you know of two or three people who could benefit from my service. Would that be all right with you?" That sets the stage early. And they may even have a couple of referrals for you right away!

Then be sure as you're working with them in the weeks and months that follow to ask them again if they know of two or three other people who could benefit from your service. It's especially effective to ask this after a customer has had something nice to say about how you have helped them. Tell them you're happy to hear that and then pop the question.

You always need to be asking for referrals. Remember that establishing, building and maintaining strong relationships with key groups contributes to your overall success and your success with personal selling.

Week 21 Action

Your task this week is to get more testimonials and referrals. Start asking customers for them at the onset, throughout and after the sales cycle. This will help you achieve a consistent flow of testimonials and referrals and to build your business through word-of-mouth marketing.

One Hot Day in Singapore

The day started much like any other day, but that day would change my life forever. On Friday, November 20, 2009, I attended a plenary conference and two workshops as part of Global Entrepreneurship Week, supported by the Association of Small & Medium Enterprises in Singapore. The speaker was Don Hutson, co-author of the New York Times no. 1 bestseller, The One Minute Entrepreneur.

During the session, Mr. Hutson talked about the importance of having a mentor, someone whom you could speak with every now and again and whose experience you could learn from. Mentoring is a less structured approach than coaching, but effective in its own way. Mr. Hutson talked about how one of the reasons why we don't ask people to be our mentor is because we're afraid they'll say no. Mr. Hutson said that, in fact, most people would be honored and might even say yes.

I had an autographed copy of Mr. Hutson's book with me at the workshop. As I looked through the pages, I found the following two One Minute Insights: "On the entrepreneurial path, few people come into your life without a reason" and "When opportunity knocks, seize it."

At the break, I walked up to Mr. Hutson, told him how much I was enjoying his workshop and asked him if he would be my mentor. It felt like time stood still. I was ready for Mr. Hutson to say "Look kid, that's just something I say at all of my talks, so stop wasting my time and take a seat!" But I didn't care. I could handle the feeling of rejection better than I could handle the feeling of never having asked. After what felt like an eternity, Mr. Hutson said yes. I was so grateful and so excited!

Mr. Hutson invited me to meet him for breakfast the following Tuesday at 7:00 A.M. We had to meet over breakfast because he had to catch a flight back to Memphis later that morning. I had only about half an hour of his time. I was planning on writing a book and I hoped that Mr. Hutson could share his own experience of having authored and/or co-authored at least a dozen books. Over breakfast he gave me some really great advice; it meant so much more coming from Mr. Hutson himself. I was hanging onto his every word, but there was one last thing I wanted to ask him. I asked him if he would co-author my book. Once again it felt like time stood still. But this time, I was ready for Mr. Hutson to say "Tom, I'd be happy to!" After what felt like an eternity, he said no, he wouldn't co-author the book, but he would be happy to write the foreword. I was so grateful and so excited!

The lesson I learned that one hot day in Singapore was that my key to success in Canada (to be curious) wasn't enough to get me where I wanted to be in Singapore. The key to my success in Singapore would require a new quality. This new quality is my last piece of advice for you:

BE COURAGEOUS.

Selected Readings

By Don Hutson
The One Minute Negotiator (with George Lucas)
The One Minute Entrepreneur (with Ken Blanchard and Ethan Willis)

By Jim Cathcart
Relationship Selling
The Acorn Principle

By Peter Legge
The Power of a Dream
Make Your Life a Masterpiece

By Dr. Tony Alessandra
The Platinum Rule for Sales Mastery
Collaborative Selling

By Michael Gerber
The E-Myth Revisited
E-Myth Mastery

By Ivan Misner, PhD
The 29% Solution (with Michelle R. Donovan)
Givers Gain: The BNI Story (with Jeff Morris)

By Timothy Ferriss
The 4-Hour Workweek

By Napoleon Hill
Think And Grow Rich

About the Author

Tom Abbott is a Singapore-based Canadian sales trainer and coach. For more than ten years, he has been working with SOHOs, SMEs and MNCs worldwide to help them increase sales.

Tom is a member of the Association of Professional Speakers Singapore, Canadian Professional Sales Association and Marketing Institute of Singapore. Tom is also President of the Rendezvous Chapter of Business Network International and serves on the Executive Committee of the International Coach Federation Singapore.

Tom has appeared in Berita Harian newspaper, Human Resources magazine, Make It Business magazine, Singapore Women's Weekly magazine and as a guest on Business Insanity Talk Radio. He is a regular contributor of sales articles published in The Singapore Straits Times newspaper and The Singapore Marketer magazine.

Index

A

B

C

D

E

F

G

I

L

M

S

T

V

Y

soho sales coaching

Services

Soho Sales Coaching, Southeast Asia's Number 1 Sales Specialist[1], was founded in 1999 and has helped SOHOs, SMEs and MNCs increase sales. The company's one-on-one sales coaching, in-house sales training, speaking engagements and sales webinars have helped clients improve in the following areas:

- Identifying and reaching target customers.
- Differentiating from competitors.
- Converting more leads into sales.

If you have been inspired by The SOHO Solution: 21 Selling Strategies For Growing Your Small Business, why not take your development to the next level? To learn more about Soho Sales Coaching's one-on-one sales coaching, in-house sales training, speaking engagements or sales webinars, please call (+65) 9814-1458 or visit www.sohosalescoaching.com.

---

1 Soho Sales Coaching is the most "liked" Southeast Asian sales coaching and sales training brand on Facebook (as of 31 March 2011).

Sales Coaching

As a sales coach for you or your sales team members, Soho Sales Coaching provides the structure and support needed to reach sales targets more quickly. We offer coaching packages that suit every business from the one-person start-up to the large sales team within an established multinational corporation.

Packages typically include: 3 (50-minute) one-on-one videoconference or teleconference calls (so you can be coached anywhere in the world) with Tom per month, 1 "integration week" with no scheduled call (so you can implement strategies and assess your progress) and email support between sessions.

There is no long-term commitment so you can stop coaching anytime, however clients typically achieve the best results after receiving coaching for between 3-6 months. Soho Sales Coaching will also provide a 100% money-back, satisfaction guarantee so there's no risk.

Soho Solo

One-on-one coaching for self-employed business owners (consultants, photographers and techies) with no employees. This package is the ideal solution for solo entrepreneurs who are great at what they do (or need help figuring things out), but struggle when it comes to sales and marketing. Tom will help you get more clients.

Soho Micro

One-on-one coaching for self-employed business owners with up to 5 employees. This package is the ideal solution for micro-entrepreneurs who are running growing businesses, but are challenged with creating sales systems and processes.

Tom will help you focus on being a business owner and not a technician.

Soho Enterprise
One-on-one coaching for a director or manager within organizations of up to 20 employees. This package is the ideal solution for leaders of established businesses who need help developing and implementing a long-term sales and marketing strategy. Tom will help you focus on being a great sales coach for your team.

Soho Sales Team
One-on-one or group coaching for sales professionals within organizations looking to get the most out of their sales teams. This package is the ideal solution for leaders looking to maximize the return on their sales training investment. Tom will provide the structure and support needed for your sales team put into action the learning acquired through training.

Sales Webinars

Our online sales seminars are an affordable and convenient alternative to conventional seminars. We've designed them to help small business owners and sales professionals increase sales through our Soho Sales Fundamentals methodology.

Reaching Customers
This webinar demonstrates the importance of understanding customer needs. In the first component, you'll learn strategies for discovering your niche and creating qualifying questions. The second component demonstrates how to uncover your prospects' greatest challenges. The third component gives

examples of the decision-making process to help you understand how and why customers buy. In the fourth component, you'll learn strategies for consistently reaching a large number of prospects. Finally, the fifth component will share the most effective ways of organizing prospecting information.

Differentiating Your Business

In this webinar you'll learn the importance of branding yourself and your business. The first component encourages you to become a product and industry expert. The second component demonstrates how your competition is helping you without even knowing it. In the third component, you'll discover what truly differentiates your brand from the competition. In the fourth component, you'll identify what your customers find most compelling about your business. Finally, the fifth component helps you answer some of the most common and difficult questions asked by customers.

Closing More Sales

This webinar shares strategies for converting more leads into sales. In the first component, you'll learn how to get in front of more decision-makers. The second component demonstrates how to ask more intelligent questions and shorten the sales cycle. The third component helps you move prospective customers to new customers and ultimately maturing clients. In the fourth component, you'll learn how proof devices can help you close more sales. Finally, the fifth component will explain what two words could overcome almost any objection.

Winning Sales Attitude

This webinar demonstrates how your relationship with yourself and others greatly impacts your sales. The first component encourages you to focus on ways to improve and avoid focusing on past mistakes. In the second component, you'll see how a negative attitude becomes a self-fulfilling prophecy and what to do about it. The third component gives examples of how personal and professional development activities improve your selling abilities. In the fourth component, you'll learn why 75% of prospective customers don't like you and how to change that. Finally, the fifth component demonstrates how only focusing on customers does more harm than good.

Measuring Sales Success

In this webinar you'll learn how to increase sales by focusing on being a sales strategist and not just a small business owner or sales professional. In the first component, you're challenged with effectively practicing work-life balance. In the second component you'll learn about the importance of spending more time in face-to-face selling situations. The third component encourages you to use records, territory and time management tools. The fourth component explores ways of improving your skills as a manager and entrepreneur. Finally, the fifth component focuses on the importance of identifying and measuring key performance indicators.

To learn more about Soho Sales Coaching's one-on-one sales coaching or sales webinars, please call (+65) 9814-1458 or visit www.sohosalescoaching.com.